Dear Reader

The writings within this book may appear unusual to you but are true to the original communications from the Etherean Travellers and the Magical Child and have not been edited to conform with conventional writing standards. They have been left unaltered out of the highest respect for Thunderbird Woman and each of the Etherean beings, who have come in love from the highest spheres in order to impart information and offer help through their messages. These are not channelled communications, but rather reflect actual experiences, conversations and dissertations. The meanings of the writings are often only fully comprehended when the book is reread. This is as the author intended.

May this book enlighten and empower you.

Chief Bill Williams
29th of July

May the Creator Bless and Give us Back our freedom and lead us To the path of late and peace and Knowing from you the Children Will Come and Return To the Light

Thunder Bird Woman

THE ETHEREAN TRAVELLERS
AND THE MAGICAL CHILD

Thunderbird Woman

Canadian Cataloguing in Publication Data

Thunderbird Woman,
    The etherean travellers and the magical child

    ISBN 1-55212-325-1

    1. Spiritual life.   I. Title.
BF1261.2.T58 1999   131   C99-911357-7

Published in Canada by:
Trafford Publishing and
Experience Cosmic Energy Publishing

E-mail: ahtmar1@CosmicEnergyExperience.com
Website: www.cosmicenergyexperience.com

TRAFFORD

This book was published "on-demand" in cooperation with Trafford Publishing.
On-demand publishing is a unique process and service of making a book available for retail sale to the public taking advantage of on-demand manufacturing and Internet web marketing.

Suite 6E - 2333 Government St., Victoria, BC, Canada V8T 4P4

Phone	250-383-6864	Toll-free	1-888-232-4444 (Canada & US)
Fax	250-383-6804	E-mail	sales@trafford.com
Web site	www.trafford.com	A DIVISION OF TRAFFORD HOLDINGS LTD.	
Trafford Catalogue #99-0075		www.trafford.com/robots/99-0075.html	

10   9   8

Cover artwork and illustrations by Thunderbird Woman

Contents

Dedication

We Are All Children Of The Universe

I want to dedicate this book with great love and affection to all my lovely children and grandchildren, and to my relations and ancestors and, most of all, to the many, many wonderful people I have encountered in my life. I wish to acknowledge also the people who have allowed me to facilitate them on their journey back to the Heavenly Home, and those who are on the earth who have allowed me to bring them closer to the Etherean Travellers and to the First, Second and Third Resurrections.

I thank those, my friends and relations from the Etherean Worlds, for having given all their wonderful information and help. First thanks to Haida, Ahtmar, James, Dr Cheng, Kiryon, Sophia, Truth and, most of all, the lovely bringer of fragrance and good hope for all mankind, Alika. Also thanks to our legal and medical advisor, Mr James.

We have put this book together for all the people who are seeking spiritual growth and greater understanding of the time they live in at this moment. This book will particularly be of great use for those who have questions about the beginning and ending of life. This, in reality, provides a most wondrous progression for your soul to continue its travels, in loving and learning, and its understanding of all etherean vibrations, frequencies and transmissions of thought and action.

It will be of interest to those who are trained to perceive their world as black and white, and are not able to see there is a gentle veil of separations which is like an early morning summer's mist that rests upon the greens of a summer's day. But never is there a division, for earth and universe and there above the etherean worlds are all connected. These veils are very fine and fragile. The veils exist between you who live upon this earth, those who live in Hada (the lower plane of learning), as well as those who come from on high. The Etherean

Travellers who have come to guide you, sojourn back and fro through these energies. This veil of vibrations exists, as well, between you and your departed loved ones.

This is for those of you who do not believe in Angels and spirit apparitions. But I would like to let you know that there are more people from the Etherean Worlds guiding your life each and every day than you could ever be aware of. These Angel and Spirit Guides come to help and guide you onto a higher path towards progression, wisdom and reflection.

However, we want you to know that those who remained earthbound and still live in mischief, would like to give you misinformation and those who live in Hada will misdirect you until you are aware. For example, they might appear in your life as a bird, a cat, a dog, a goat, a horse, a lion, a bear, and the eagle in the sky. Since everything upon earth has a form of telepathic communication with you, if you are unconcerned and you follow their advice they will instil in you improper thoughts and ideas, and you may act upon them. Your soul will tell you to be loving, caring and honest, but your oversoul will insist that you give in to your lying, stealing, or worse.

Whatever the Etherean Worlds have brought down to your earth—the red planet—has that vibration, that love, and knowledge of communication with one another. Remember that when you look at your pet, if you have one, and try to experiment with it. Try to exchange thoughts. Be patient. You will find out quickly that the animals, which have higher vibrations and frequencies, are not such lowly creatures.

The same kind of telepathic communication exists between you and your Angel Guides, or your Spirit Guides, from the Etherean Worlds. It happens many times between husbands and wives, brothers and sisters, or friends. A parent may be in one part of the world and the child in another, and yet they will have information about each other that is quite astoundingly accurate. Yes, telepathic communication is possible between whatever liveth upon the earth. Didn't it say in the scriptures, "Go to the beasts upon the field and ask them?" Go to the ancients, to the Native Peoples, and ask them. They will tell you that the rocks they use are the bones of the earth and they have either positive or negative feelings, and they have also understanding and vibrations. Everything that exists in the Universe has this magnificent vibration that comes from the Etherean Worlds.

Foreword

A Message From Thunderbird Woman And The Etherean Travellers

The
Etherean
Travellers
and the
Magical
Child

I am known as Thunderbird Woman and came to earth as a Magical Child from the Etherean Worlds, accompanied by my friends, the Etherean Travellers. We bring to the earthlings a message of peace and change towards a new millennium, where all nations join hands in return to the belief in one Great Spirit—their Creator.

We have noticed that here, on the red planet—planet earth—you are living in a constant state of war and anger, but have a hunger for spirituality. The gentle ones amongst you, they too need to become wise. The words 'love' or "I am so spiritual" are very cheaply created words when they cannot be applied to all of humanity, as well as all that lives upon your earth.

We have noticed that wars you allowed or have created are still being fought upon your ancient battlefields. The spirits of the men and women who fought in the wars are trapped in your earthly atmospherea. We have also come into a realisation that your words of love and consideration, are like a very thin veneer which you have never been able to break through to realize that to make a war, it takes two. And in the words of the old Mahatma, he said, "Truly that it takes two to pick up the rifle, the bomb or the gun, or the chemical missile to send to one another to create havoc and destruction. It is not perceived within the twisted minds and hearts full of greed of those who earn their livings by creating their tools of war, that this cannot continue."

For you who live in an illusion, we would like you, this moment, to become aware that when one proclaims he comes to defend you, and his protection comes at a very high price, it may devastate your spiritual and economic existence and it will create losses of all life. For this war must at all costs be prevented, for the after-effects worldwide will tilt your earth, and some of you may experience a new tomorrow.

Do not fall into the trap of eastern religions for you will not return here once more. Be aware, all producers of food, that discarding food and survival supplies is robbing the elders from going into a peaceful tomorrow and taking away the happiness and innocence of children. This earth belongs to no one who wanders upon its crust. You're here all to spiritually progress, to overcome hatred and greed, and have a heart full of understanding and forgiveness for each and every one.

We foretell that when you are done with your earthly journey, you are the one who will come before the judges of the First Resurrection and you will judge yourself and you will experience that which you have done to others. So our advice is intended to give you a more aware spiritual journey and an awakening for everyone.

Acknowledgements

I began writing this book in the summer of 1959. Over the years, a number of people read my manuscript and/or worked with me to transcribe it. I wish to thank the following people for their kind assistance: Maureen Samuels, Matilda Bisang and Robert Eighteen-Bisang, Josane, Howard, Barbara Deodat, Natalie Dunser, Chris Scott and Ami Scott.

A special thanks to Jon Andrasz, Joan Sutherland and Patti Ballin for their wonderful support in making it possible for this book to be published. Also, thank you to Rex Weyler for his help and encouragement.

A warm thank you to my friend, Katharina Watson, for all her wonderful hard work and support and for her understanding of those from the Etherean Worlds.

Chapter 1

The Magical Birth

I descended from the Etherean Worlds and so received a body that was stillborn. The medical personnel, nuns and custodial family who were present when I arrived, witnessed the strange non-birth of my being. So read on, my friend, and you will come to know and hopefully appreciate my being upon this earth. Many blessings and so it be.

Now make yourselves comfortable and I will begin to tell you this story by going back approximately twenty years before I came to earth.

My custodial mother was a North American Indian from the MicMac nation who lived in Europe. She married a young man who was from a blue-blood, industrialist family, and he was their only son. They were very well known and very wealthy—considered in those

The
Etherean
Travellers
and the
Magical
Child

days as an upper-class family. These were people who lived in a palace-like estate with 128 rooms.

Before they met, the custodial father was sent to a seminary to become a Jesuit priest. During an Easter celebration, a fairground was set up in town. When the fairground was making its happy sounds and the smells of cotton candy and donuts wafted over the walls of the seminary, the young man did hear the sounds and did smell the scents. It awoke a desire in him to scale the walls and journey into town. Here he met a tremendously beautiful young woman who stood out in the crowd. Although she was chaperoned, they quickly fell in love and decided to marry. This was against his family's wishes because of the complications of race differences and, of course, since he was leaving the priesthood.

The lady who gave birth to this body of mine was herself a spiritually evolved person who was very gifted. She had abilities that had been handed down from generations of ancestors to her and was therefore totally out of sync living in the land called The Netherlands (Holland). Was she born there? Was she taken there when she was very small? I do not know. What I do know is that a large number of people spoke of her with immense love, compassion and gratitude. And some said that she was a MicMac princess. Her name was also MicMac—Marett MicMac. Now, I say with great thankfulness that she was a MicMac. I say this because she handed me the values and belief system she had been taught, and gave the existence and the voyage to the body that I am living in.

MicMac was told seven years before I was to be born that a Magical Child was going to come through her and that the child would be a messenger of change and peace. At the time when she found herself to be pregnant, again she was made aware of the coming of this Magical Child. As a result, from as early as 6 months of age, I was called the Magical Child. But alas, back to the birth, back to the journey of why I came to live in this body on this earth plane.

Well, as you are all sitting here around me, smiling and listening to the story, let us continue moving through the events that manifested themselves in the city of Rotterdam, Holland. Why was this city where I began my journey called Rotterdam? I do not know. Maybe it has a significance that I cannot explain at the moment. All I know is that these two people, who were to become my custodial parents, were visiting there because they owned a number of fairground attractions with which they travelled around. Can you smell the cotton candy? Can you hear the music of the organ, the stereo systems of the day - by that I mean "mono" sound systems? Can you hear the laughter and the happy chatter of the children? Can you hear the ringing of the bells of the streetcars and the sounds of the automobiles passing by? My custodial parents also owned a number of hotels, including the Kurehouse Hotel in Den Haag located on the ocean shoreline of Scheveningen, and had interests in beer breweries such as Three Horseshoe Beers. In addition, they manufactured woollens for the army and navy.

And these custodial parents knew at that time that there was uncertainty on this earth in which they would be involved, but nobody knew the outcome and what the restlessness of the governments would bring upon them. They were seriously concerned but not totally understanding. This was in the early throes of World War II. You might ask why this should be so important. Let me assure you that you will find out as we go on. It has again to do with the Etherean Travellers and their love and affection for this Magical Child.

By now do you wonder what makes me so magical? Come; let's find out. Marett MicMac had been taken to the Queen Elizabeth Hospital, a Catholic hospital, because it was her due time. Or was it her overdue time? I do not know. In the birthing room, along the one wall, was a long, grey-black granite counter with a large bowl. Leaning in it was another bowl in which, I suppose, they bathed the babies. There was also a sink where people washed their hands, and around it were yellow ceramic tiles with black edges. The floor was black-and-white granite with a drainage hole that made hosing down easy. A clock was mounted on the right wall. Lights with large, old-fashioned glass shades around the light bulbs, and enamel-covered metal shades on top, were suspended from the ceiling. There was no such fancy medical equipment as doctors and nurses are using today! No, No! It was still quite simple then. And then there was a big iron bed. The custodial mother was in it. The people in the room were working very hard. Some of the nurses were nuns, and in those days they had mid-wives to assist with the birth. The custodial mother was becoming very concerned as she had been in labour pains for a long, long time. The medical staff was rushing back and forth and started to get worried. Finally, they were discussing the possibility that this child was not going to be saved and even that the custodial mother might not be.

We were standing there—Ahtmar, James and myself—watching this poor lady and feeling compassionate as she was suffering. "You are saying that you were watching," you ask. "Were you not the baby about to be born?" And some people would say, "That's normal, that was just your conscience that was outside of the body." But that was not quite so. You see, I had come down from the Etherean Worlds with my Etherean Travellers who urged me at that time, "Watch what is happening, for this little body coming into the world will be yours so you may understand the human world." Now, let us look at this together. This lady was about to give birth to this body that would become mine under very difficult circumstances. By now the doctors were in a big hurry and, although they pulled and adjusted and did everything they could, the little body did not appear. Thinking that the baby would be suffocating in the birth canal, they applied forceps and started to pull at the baby's head. And as the baby finally came forward it appeared lifeless. No sound was coming from it, so they started to smack the baby and massage it but to no avail as the baby was dead. My custodial mother remembered what had been foretold to her about my arrival and asked the nurses to wrap the baby and keep it in the birthing room. The nuns, doctors and nurses had noticed strange things happening in the room. Many little lights and colours were seen floating about. They also heard the tinkling of tiny bells.

Some 5 hours had passed when one of my Etherean friends said, "Go in there now, this is your time. Go and take your body before it cools off too much. Hurry! Hurry!" Next, I felt a gentle push and before I knew what was happening, I was in the baby's body feeling very, very cramped and somewhat uneasy. A miracle was declared as the baby came back to life. I didn't know what to do to adjust, and I don't know that I can say that I have ever become comfortable being in this body. I have had lots of difficulties.

A Baby's Cry

A baby cries so new is its arrival,
It cries on and on,
Oh, his soul remembers its heavenly home from where it came,
Now angels will come and console till heavenly home's memory is
     gone,
And baby is on earth, really home!

The custodial mother was not so very happy I suppose, for she had finally given birth but not, as she later said, to her own child. The baby was then wrapped in a blanket and given to the custodial mother. I remember looking around and feeling a little bit in despair. Oh, I felt lost. My Etherean Travellers stayed close and assured me that yes, it would be all right for a while. The more they tried to comfort me, the more uncomfortable I was feeling, noticing at the same time that I was unable to leave this body at this time. And they finally convinced me to stay and told me that it was necessary for the earth that I remained.

At that moment, after all I wondered, why should I stay here for the earth? If it was to continue like this, it felt like it was going to be very difficult. The Etherean Travellers reassured me that they would always stay close to me as my companions—as they always have. And of course, this book is also dedicated out of thanks to my most beloved companions from the Spirit World—my Etherean Travellers—who are protecting and loving me and who have guided me through many, many perilous situations in my life.

The custodial parents also had a ten-year-old son who was not very happy with the new arrival. In fact, he was quite angry and jeal-

The
Etherean
Travellers
and the
Magical
Child

ous of me as we were growing up, since he could not understand how I could move things at will and make them disappear and reappear. Furthermore, I wasn't the little boy this family had hoped for. The difficulty and frustration it caused for them to have this child (who they said was not a child) was extreme, since I was so different from other children. They often complained that they had a thousand-year-old being in a child's body. So I have to explain to you that it was very difficult for the Magical Child growing up.

However, there was more to it than that. As time went on, this little child proved difficult to deal with and was in many ways not like the others. It seems that the Magical Child did not play like other children. She had a desire to play but other children did not understand her. There were not necessarily physical differences because she was actually a nice looking child. She had beautiful big, dark blue-eyes, thick blond hair, and a gold-toned, well-proportioned body. It was the energy around the body that continually seemed to trigger problems. The adult world wasn't very happy with her either because the Magical Child would say things to them that they were not very appreciative of. She sometimes wanted to discuss things that were very advanced for her age. She knew things, and she said very unusual things. This child had a strange kind of power that they did not understand and often feared.

But let us go back briefly to the moment of birth. When the body came forth the head of the baby was covered with a veil, which is called the helm or kol, in some countries, and is also known under different names in others. When they removed it, they noticed that this veil had seven corners. It is told that, as they rolled it onto a silver pin, it was shining and it sent off sparks. It was put into a container with Frankincense and Myrrh and given to a lady named Dora Dillon. I would do anything to find this person or her children. I have no idea if she is still on this earth plane, but I am sure that she would remember who I am, or at least, who my custodial mother was.

As of today, I have not been able to find out where the custodial parents had been married. Sadly enough, the custodial mother was in my life only for a very short time. My custodial father was there only sparsely. However, I cannot say that he was without love or compassion, for he was indeed a gentle soul and he did care in his own way.

They also had two other children—a son, whom I mentioned earlier, and a daughter who was 20 years older than I. Apparently, this daughter was pregnant at the same time as my custodial mother was expecting me and gave birth to her daughter before my custodial mother did. I know very little about these people, because the amount of contact I have had with them over the years was so minimal. And the last time we met, I was told very many things about the Magical Child.

But back to my story. So here we have a child growing up rapidly not knowing where it belonged in this world, or why it was that nothing felt right or seemed to fit as it should. At the age of about one-and-one-half years, the first serious incident happened. My custodial parents owned a pleasure boat on which they would travel along the canals in Holland. One day, while they were having their morning coffee, I, the little child, who had been left unattended, found an opportunity to crawl out of my enclosure onto the boat, and subsequently fell overboard. As I was floating in the water (because my Etherean Travellers had kept the body in such a manner that it would not sink) a delivery boy came by and noticed me. In total panic he reached out and was able to grasp part of my clothing and pull me to safety. I myself had been standing ashore watching this body bob up and down in the water. Then I went to hover over the boat to look around some more. I thought it quite interesting, especially when they took the body out of the water, gave it a warm bath and rubbed it down, waiting for a response. It was very tragic from the human perspective and it would have severely distressed my parents had I not gone back into the body.

My journey on earth, watched over by the lovely beings from the Etherean Worlds who come from the Higher Resurrections to serve mankind as Guides, Protectors and as Angels, continued. The next major incident happened at the age of three when my custodial mother was discovered to have tuberculosis. In desperation, she was taken to the hospital in a city called Purmerend, in Holland. As she went I knew what was happening; I understood that never again was she

The
Etherean
Travellers
and the
Magical
Child

going to return. A gentle good-bye was whispered and then I was left behind. During visiting hours I was not allowed in to see her but had to stay with the nuns downstairs in the hospital. Naturally, they thought they were dealing with a regular child, another human, and were acting accordingly. Two nuns had sat me on the counter and started talking to me. One said to the other: "Isn't she pretty, isn't she a lovely child?" The other asked me, "Wouldn't you like to become a nun?" to which I replied, "No, I don't want to become a nun." They asked me what I would want to become. "Oh," I answered, "it was already decided who I was going to be when this body was larger, but I had a long time to wait." Then they asked me if I knew what was happening to my custodial mother. "My mama is very ill" I answered, "and soon she will go back to the Etherean Worlds. They will take her Home, you know." The two nuns looked at each other in surprise. One said, "Yes, yes she will go to Heaven." The other nun said, "How sad for her, she is only so small." I told them that they did not need to feel sorry for me; that I understood. Nevertheless, they lifted me off the counter and took me to the statue of the mother Mary, thinking that she would be the one who would console me.

Only many, many years later did I discover that my devotion was directed back to the one who had given me life, to the one who is called the Great Spirit, the Great God of Light, the Light that is soft and gentle and can make musical tones and colours; that was the one I was praying to whereas the others were praying to the statue.

And as time went by, I was developing more and more in my spiritual growth. It was discovered that I also had contracted tuberculosis and was taken to the city called Den Haag while my custodial mother was being buried in Purmerand. I was, therefore, not physically in the same city where her burial took place. Later, people experienced a tremendous shock when I described to them exactly the route along which they had taken her to the burial ground. Their bewilderment was expressed with statements like, "You were not in the city when she was buried and there is no one here who could have told you. How could you possibly have information like that?" I did not say very much to them because they did not comprehend. But I felt sad then, as I do now, because these people did not understand that they were living in a world of many dimensions.

I would just like to mention here that the lovely person, who was my custodial mother and who gave birth to this body, is now in the Etherean World and has made tremendous progress there.

After my recovery I moved to a city called Shertogenbos where my Etherean Friends started to come and educate me during night-time hours. This went on for quite a while. And at age four, when the situation with the war was really starting to come into full picture, they used to tell me to watch what these humans do and say. "We will preserve you," they would tell me. "We will watch over you." Meanwhile I was being moulded more and more into this human body, having to become like them. It was a very difficult journey not being able to really understand them, and also being able to read people's thoughts and their desires, for I was on a different frequency. It was also quite painful to try to forget where I came from and to adjust to this strange life, the very colourful life these people were living. The memory is painful because the Etherean Home is so lovely, so warm, so beautiful. How can people ever forget? And yet, many people do and for a while, it seems, I did too. But not really.

May the Great God of Light bless you. Well, I just wished you a blessing from the Etherean Worlds, and this blessing can come to you in many colours, sounds and wishes. It is a blessing I often utter when things are very difficult to remember and the pain of loneliness is so great.

Before my custodial mother passed on, she had hired a new housekeeper whose husband had died of tuberculosis, thinking that this fact would make the woman a very understanding person. Well, loyal to the household she was, but loving, no. She actually caused a lot of pain and needless suffering. So did the young man who called himself my brother. No, this family was not very close. It was a very strange, loose-hinged situation. But I do forgive them and, of course, I do feel great sorrow and I send them thoughts of love. What choice do we have? There will be a day when we will meet again.

As I was telling you, the war was on and the town I was now

The
Etherean
Travellers
and the
Magical
Child

living in received the heaviest bombardments anywhere in the Netherlands. People around me were hungry and cold. The hunger was not as great as the cold. The coal wagons would roll through the city to the hospital and to the buildings where the Germans—who were the oppressors—were residing.

The German occupation was a very disastrous situation. However, this family unit was protected. The people around me did not understand why they often had a feeling as if someone was watching over them. As the bombs and the grenades came down and exploded, we moved about in an effort to keep safe. One day, the suggestion was made that we should seek shelter in a nearby shoe factory, and the housekeeper was sent out to enquire. As she was coming closer to the gate of the factory she experienced a strange feeling. At the same time it seemed as if a very powerful hand was pulling her back and she heard a voice saying: "No, don't go in." So she turned around and went back to the house where she told what had happened. Obviously, the woman was in tune with Spirit. No doubt about it, Spirit had taken a good hold on her.

Hearing the housekeeper's story the others agreed after much discussion not to go to the shoe factory. They decided instead to look for another place. Many times I asked myself: "Why did they not just stay in the house? The house was safe. It was protected by the Etherean Worlds." However, they were not sufficiently in tune with the Angels and the Spirit World and wanted to leave because they considered it unsafe. Just at that time, a carpenter friend happened to come by and told them about the small house he and his father were living in. His father had reinforced the basement with great, big wooden beams and he had built wooden crypts along the walls for people to sleep in. As a result, all the members of my household decided to move to this tiny house. Can you imagine, leaving a house that was built out of brick and concrete and had a beautiful, strong basement to go and stay with these humble people in their little house that was reinforced by trees? So, we all went to this house and rushed to the basement. Soon the bombing and shelling started around us. Suddenly, an enormous sound of a bomb heading towards earth was heard and then it was quiet. "It stopped" said the housekeeper. "It will hit the shoe factory." They then heard this loud explosion. Hundreds of people died instantly in the shoe factory where they thought they would be safe.

Then the housekeeper had an idea and blurted out, "Do you think it is going to hit here?" She had barely uttered the words when they heard another loud crash and the whole top of the house was blown off. And then there was nothing left. The door that had separated them from whatever was going on outside, flew open. Dust and dirt swirled in. They all looked at each other and someone uttered: "Thank God, thank God for at least we are all still alive." They crawled upstairs and looked around, and saw that nothing was left above the foundation. And they came to the understanding that it was only through a miracle that they had survived. My custodial father, in fact, told people that so long as the Magical Child was there, they would survive. Next, they decided to find protection in the war bunkers of the hospital and, after gathering some food, that's where they went.

They were busy settling themselves in one of the bunkers and, while all that commotion was going on, they lost me. Everyone assumed that I was with someone else. Nobody tried to find out where I really was. The sirens sounded again. The war went into action once more. Heavy fighting had resumed and I found myself outside as the grenades were exploding around me. I walked up to a building and could barely reach the handle of the door. I pushed the door open, looked inside, and came to the realization that there were bodies stacked up along the walls, high up to the ceiling, and some were laid out on wooden slats.

And then I had a special encounter. I saw a beautiful little child standing there, dressed in a white gown, while her dead body was laying on one of the slabs. I called out to her and told her not to worry, reassuring her that her family was safe somewhere in the bunkers and that she should go back with her Angel to the Etherean World. Don't linger, don't linger, I told her. The Angels will take you home.

Meanwhile a nun had walked up to me and wanted to know if I wasn't afraid, and did I not realise that it was very dangerous out

*The
Etherean
Travellers
and the
Magical
Child*

there. I told her that I did not think it was dangerous for me and said: "Don't you see? I have my friends with me. They are taking care of me. They really take care, you know." But she did not understand that the ones I was speaking of were the Etherean Travellers who had been with me from the beginning. To look for our families, she took me from bunker to bunker. Suddenly I heard my father's voice, "There she is! She is okay. You see, she is with one of the Sisters. Nothing happened to her." And he added, "It seems strange that nothing ever happens to her, wherever she is it seems to be safe. While she was walking around, many buildings here were flattened. She doesn't appear to be bothered by it at all and seems to feel that it is all right. We don't understand where she gets this feeling of being safe from." Then he paused to contemplate a little and finally said, "I remember how we were told that we would have this Magical Child and that somehow the Etherean Worlds have a special mission for her. So I suppose nothing bad will happen to her. She will survive the war. She survived diphtheria, the tuberculosis that took her custodial mother, and she has also survived so many other critical events. At times we thought she would not make it because she was so sickly, yet she pulled through time and time again."

Life continued, spring came anew, and the war was still on. It was decided to open the fair grounds in an effort to create a little happiness in the midst of so much depression and to make it easier to get through the war. My custodial father brought some beer from his brewery, built a large dance floor, and added music.

My custodial father was a member of the underground where he used me to help people survive and escape from the Germans. I gave information for their safe movement, predicted bombing and SS house raids, and pinpointing locations for radio transmitters. He nearly got caught himself when the Germans came banging on the door looking for him and demanded entry into the house. The house was surrounded and there was nowhere else to go. On this occasion, he and the housekeeper opened up the bed boards beneath the mattress on my bed and he crawled in. I lay on top of the mattress and stayed there until the search was over. So, it was a terrible time, a time of fear and of noise. What I found very scary were the beams of the large search lights that were floating through the sky, looking like huge fingers coming down. For some reason or other, it did not feel good to me. The lights would come and when they left, it felt much darker than before.

It was thought that the people needed some entertainment and a break from this war, so a fair ground was organised. Everybody contributed. One brought ice cream from his restaurant, others brought all kinds of baked goods and other food. The people could find relief when the music would come out between the bombings, and they were able to dance at night until another siren forced a halt to the festivities as everyone sought shelter.

One sometimes questions people's reasoning in coping with the war. Some were very, very afraid and did nothing else but repeat the same prayers over and over again. On the other hand, there were those who were seeking to help as many people as possible to survive the war. It was during this time that my custodial father brought in a few house trailers. There was one which was particularly large that had two bedrooms, a living room, a large kitchen, bathrooms and showers. It was totally equipped like a miniature house and I was very excited since it was intended for shelter between the bombings. Even after negotiations to stop the bombing finished, we continued to live in this trailer for some time.

Ode to Jehovih

The universe was generated by thought,
Movements of moon and stars,
A firmament was celebrated between heavens and earth like
            stars Saturn, Earth, Jupiter, and great Mars,
Are pointers of days and nights where all created sun, moon, stars
New appointers days and nights, light and dark with tides of
            oceans ebb and flood,
Now ruling man's emotions all times,
Ode to the ruler of all mortal beings, a beloved Great God of Light.

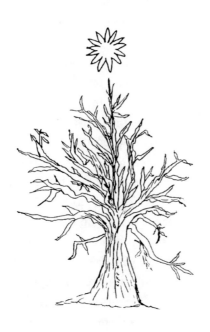

Chapter 2

A Discourse On A Holy Tree

And it was in here, in the trailer, that my friend from the Etherean World came to do some serious teaching. One evening, while I was asleep in my bed, someone touched my shoulder. "Wake up," he whispered. "We cannot let you neglect your lessons. I have come to teach you, for there are no others. It will be quiet as I show you the lessons you must learn. Later, much later, you will pass on these lessons to the people so they may understand how the Etherean Worlds and the earth are to operate." As he stood there, he held an enormous book in his hands. He started to read out of it, little by little, interspersed by explanations. On a big board he drew a magnificent tree which he called the Tree of Life. It was the Tree of Good and Evil, meaning good and evil decisions and choices which people make. My lovely visitor came wearing a mantle in a soft colour outlined with gold. He had the loveliest, most gentle face and his name was Mr James.

He came back every night for a long, long time to teach me what he said was very important. The people around me began to wonder why I appeared constantly tired and why I was falling asleep at the breakfast table. And why was I always mumbling something they could not comprehend? One night, when the visitor came to study with me out of his enormous, wonderful book, again I discovered something. As I looked over the edge of the bed, I saw for the first time that this person from the Etherean Worlds had no legs. "How come you have no legs?" I shouted in surprise, seeing him floating in the air. By now I had become accustomed to the limitations of the physical body and gotten used to the idea that, when you touched something, it was quite solid. However, any time I had touched the person from the Etherean Worlds, he was either solid or misty, but this time he had no legs! The fear I experienced at that moment triggered a memory, but not soon enough or strong enough to set my mind back to reasoning and to understanding how the Etherean Worlds really operate. Coming to earth consumes a great amount of energy and if the oxygen levels here are not sufficient, the Spirit and Angel worlds have to make do in whatever way they can. Sometimes, they can only partially materialize as a result.

I shall now talk to you about the Tree of Life and you too will understand the mystery of the Etherean Worlds. For it should not be a mystery to any of you who live here on earth. And yet, it was imparted only to a few like myself. The mystery of the Tree of Life was explained to me many, many times, making sure that my physical self was programmed in also. This ensured that I could hand down to you what I was taught.

One night, after leafing through the beautiful pages of his enormous book, Mr James, the Etherean Traveller, turned it around and held it leaning against his body. He encouraged me to move closer so that I could see better. When I did, I saw on one page a magnificent tree. It was a huge, old tree. He said that the tree was millions of years old. This tree offers mankind the power of understanding, and it gives mankind a moment to sit still and to ponder the why, when, where, and how they should be living. Now I know, amongst you, are many who will say, "Aha! Religion!" No, this is not about religion, but about each one of you and your Spirituality. He took me to the very roots of the Tree of Life, and beneath, and then continued up through the trunk to the branches to look at the fruits, and finally we reached its top. What was so peculiar about this tree was its tip, the part of the tree that is reaching straight up, shining like a magnificent light.

I know that many people have heard about the Tree of Life. So they went and traced their ancestry, sat down, studied it, and declared that they had a family tree.

Well, the Tree of Life is something else. It speaks about the paths in life of which there are many that can be taken to reach the Etherean Worlds. However, there is basically only one path—straight up. This is your path if you are Spiritual and you have a clear conscience and a pure heart. The difficulty is that this is what makes it so hard for many to understand, or believe.

Maybe stirring up the memory deep within you will help to bring yourself back upon a path of understanding about how you should reach out for that final pinnacle on top of the tree so you will find what is programmed into your subconscious mind by your soul.

Of course, many ancient civilisations knew about the Tree of Life long before the Babylonians and long before the Egyptian pyramids. Oh yes, even before Atlantis—a long time before. The Tree of Life is a knowledge upon the earth for all mankind that is to be shared with one another. The Tree of Life is the knowledge of right and wrong that man understands and should be aiming for within himself.

Now, stand up for a minute and try something. Imagine you are a tree. Hold your arms out to the side. Wave them back and forth, from the side to the front, up and down, and let your hands hang a little. Are you standing straight? What does it feel like standing there and waving in the wind like a tree? You too, who are living in tepees that are stacked upon each other many, many floors high. Yes, stand there. It is, of course, better for you if you are on the main floor with no basement underneath. This gives the best grounding to what you

The
Etherean
Travellers
and the
Magical
Child

are feeling. But what I would really like you to do one day is journey into the forest or into the park and stand next to a tree. Stand there very quietly. Have your arms hanging loosely and allow your body to relax. Really let go. Then hug the tree and close your eyes and imagine what it feels like to be a tree. Exchange your energy with the tree, for we are all linked. See how it feels to be something else, to have a different energy.

Now let's go back to the journey through the Tree of Life my Etherean Friend is going to take you on. We shall see if you have a greater understanding of the final journey when you have gone through this tree—a journey for which you need to prepare yourself before you leave this earth. Similarly, if you go to Hawaii, Mexico, France, Egypt, or to the Baltic Seas, to the Himalayas or anywhere else in the world, you will pack a suitcase containing appropriate footwear and comfortable clothing, according to the climate. Think for a moment about all the things you would do to prepare yourself to go on a trip. You are probably asking yourself, "What is she getting at? Where is she taking me? Why is she talking about this?" Well, my Etherean Traveller said that you take greater care in preparing your itinerary for your travels here on earth than you take for time in reflection, and for peace and harmony to prepare yourself for the greatest travel of your life—the journey that takes you back to the Etherean Worlds. Shouldn't you be prepared for it? Shouldn't you learn what the Tree of Life is all about? When you start your Etherean Journey with your wonderful Etherean Friends to go back Home, whether it is instant or whether it is slow, wherever you are, shouldn't you be prepared?

I am going to give you a few moments to think about this. Are you realising that you need to be prepared? Have you come to this conclusion? Of course you have. You have come to understand that something ought to change in your life and that it is not others who have to make the change. It is you, the seeker, you who lives in the body that needs to change. As my Etherean Traveller explained to me, the following information needs to be handed down to you.

We are standing in front of this enormous tree looking at it. The fruits upon the tree of your labour are your thoughts and the energy that you put into loving the Etherean Worlds to prepare yourself. If you step closer to the tree, you can see the roots. Are they well rooted in the earth? Yes, indeed, they are, but in a way that they can still move somewhat within the earth to get oxygen, water supply and all the minerals and nutrients the tree needs to maintain itself. Have you done that for yourself? Do you sometimes sit still to contemplate and have your roots resting? Do you meditate and do some deep breathing? Nourishment is thinking about the Spirit that you are. After all, that is what you are first—Spirit. Now wait a moment; think about that! Are you really Spirit, or are you one of those who think that when they pass away that that is the end? Have you ever a surprise coming! No, it will be your new beginning.

"For instance," the Etherean Traveller said, "there is no death for anyone. When you come down from your Creator, you have clearly made your decision to come upon the earth. You were granted this journey down here for your learning. What are you here to learn? Not how to be self-centred or egotistical or how to gain huge amounts of money. That is not what it is about. If you became very wealthy by decree, as some of you have, it was meant for you to be the biggest lesson of all. A lesson as to how you can share your fortune in the Universe with causes or individuals who are having a difficult time, and how you can learn to care with much greater capacity of love than those who came upon the earth placed in unfortunate situations. It is also teaching you the lesson on how to be free. The difference here is between one whom had a cradle that stood in a palace and one who had a cradle that stood in a poor house. It wasn't the Etherean Worlds that created the journey. It was you that made this choice."

For instance, a man by the name of Ari Onassis, who thought himself very intelligent, was upon the earth. He gained enormous amounts of money and power. However, it seems that what he did with his power could not have been very harmonious or very good because now there is only one person left living in this man's family. All the others have returned Home, leaving no legacy other than mounds of money—enormous amounts of wealth. Can you imagine

29

*The
Etherean
Travellers
and the
Magical
Child*

that his daughter, Tina Onassis, with all her money, was in much need of love, compassion, understanding and spirituality, but was not able to buy it. In fact, the money got in the way of attracting truly loving, caring and kind friends. You see, I tell you this so you can contemplate for a moment what it is you want with this money. What is the attraction to all these earthly material things? Why is it given to you and not to the next person? The answer is that your lesson is a considerably greater one to learn than that of those who have nothing much to show for themselves.

"I thought you were speaking of the Tree of Life," I hear you say. Yes my friend, you are climbing very gently upon the tree. If I were you, I would attempt not to slip off. So many of you are running around, wanting to attain great Spirituality. Are you attaining your Spirituality by trying this and that and by going from guru to guru? Have they given you what they have? "They have not!" you say. Keep climbing, keep climbing, while you ponder about this.

Imagine that you went to all these gurus, whomever they are, and you sit with this one and you chant with that one. For whom are you chanting? Why are you chanting? Do you think you are becoming Spiritual? Are you praying to this Guru so he or she shall save you? What a fool you are! You see, at this moment, the Etherean Traveller is bringing you higher and higher up the tree and you will be experiencing the many branches. Oh, you interrupt again, asking me, "You are not going to give us the answer as to how we should do it?" Well, my Etherean Friend is wanting you to do the travelling. Why should he do it for you? He already has travelled from the Etherean Worlds down here to make you understand this Tree of Life.

I can hear one of you mumbling, "I am ill, so very ill." Are you ill because of what you did? Are you ill because of the non-understanding of your parents or are you ill because of hatred? Are you confused? Do you live in a sphere of anger? Or do you feel ill of Spirit? You see, my friend, there are so many illnesses and there can be so much imbalance. But let me see, maybe we can impart to you some suggestions for your healing. Yes, I can hear you laugh and say, "Oh yeah, some suggestions for healing all right." Well, we just may give you that.

*The
Etherean
Travellers
and the
Magical
Child*

Go to your bathroom, fill your tub with lukewarm water and lay in it. Stay there for three-to-four minutes. You may even have a bath there, if you wish, but make sure that absolutely all the soap residue is rinsed off your body. Now turn the tap on to make the water as hot as you possibly can stand it. Let this hot water stream over your body. Good. Step out of the tub and take a large towel or a housecoat and wrap it around you. Walk from your bathroom to the southern-most corner of your house, your apartment or your tepee. Now take the towel off and make one turn clockwise, then one turn counter-clockwise and another one clockwise again. Wrap yourself back in the towel, go to your bed and cover yourself up so you become very warm. As you do this, I want you to continually stay in touch with what is in your Spirit—stay in touch with who you really are. Fine, you are sensing what the body feels—warm, cold. After ten minutes, out of the bed you come and repeat the same ritual all over again (no need to soap yourself this time). We are going to repeat this ritual seven times.

"What will all this do for me?" I can hear you ask. Well, you see, we are going to bring you in touch with the body and Spirit. You will understand that, as the tree is standing there made of wonderful wood, water and minerals, it has also its own Spirit within. So, in order to get you back in touch with your Spirituality and to have you regain your balance with the Etherean Worlds, we will repeat this seven times a day for seven days.

You are saying, "I don't understand this. What is it that the both of them (the Etherean Traveller and the Magical Child) want?" What they want is to impart to you a Higher Consciousness.

Let us think for a moment as you are now sitting on one of the branches of the Tree of Life. You may have thought that the trip to India you had planned was going to do it, and you are sitting pretty. Someone else is sitting on another branch who thinks that the practice of yoga will get him there. The trip to India or Egypt, the practice of yoga, the visit to the Taj Mahal—none of these are getting you there. But you may try, if you like. Every time you are with such a belief on a branch of the tree, eventually you will have to climb back down to the trunk. Don't you see that this would be a waste of your energy?

The
Etherean
Travellers
and the
Magical
Child

It would be much better to climb from the trunk directly to the Etherean Worlds, to your Higher Consciousness, to the Great God of Light.

And every time you arrive at a branch, whether it is called Judaism, Catholicism, Protestantism, New Ageism, Budhism or whatever all the 'isms' are called, eventually you will have to go back to the centre, to the trunk of the Tree of Life, in order to be able to reach the top, to reach the pinnacle. Of course, we are going to journey with you so that you can come to understand.

I hear one of you saying, "I was such an unhappy person, I suffered so much hardship." Have you? Why have you? Well, if you really have, I will ask you to give me your definition of what happiness means. I will tell you. Happiness is the experience which you know after the pain and the suffering. The greater the suffering, the greater the happiness when it comes. Remember, the lesson here is not to become bitter, hateful or angry during your suffering (or your proclaimed suffering) so that when happiness wants to come, it will not be kept out of your soul. Think about this. After all, you are climbing upon the Tree of Life to find that which is good and kind, and which is harmonious to you.

My Etherean Traveller said that, by the time you reach the trunk of the Tree of Life, you will have come to a much greater understanding as to who you are. This I truly believe. Let us pause for another moment and reflect. Reflect on the things that you did for yourself or the things you have done for others, and the things that you have done to others.

I hear someone saying, "Some Ethereal Child this is! She is forgetting that we all did some suffering, including herself." No, but I want you to get to a point of enormous growth as we have discussed already. Do you know for sure that you never, ever caused anyone pain? Let us take a serious look at it. Pray for those you have hurt and ask for forgiveness so that you can hand it to the Angels. They will take it up to the Etherean Worlds.

And Mr James said, "I know that some people cannot understand that there are Angels." "You mean that I could go upon a path to be an Angel?" I ask. "Yes, you can too," he said. "At times of dis-ease you might see me and it might appear to you as if I had wings. You look a little surprised because I have never, ever come to you in the form of a being with wings. Well, let's see how one can come to be existing as one of those who are said to be beings with wings—because you have seen them—though you question yourself why you yourself have not had wings here on earth. Well, we shall analyse it all, my child, for yourself and for you to also tell others so that they may understand." There is much to be given and passed on to all the people who are in a state of confusion or fear because of their religious belief. One day soon—one day very soon—when the time comes, you and I, together with all the other Etherean Travellers and with all the Angels, shall be able to show them that we are not far away and that people can reach us by telepathic communication. If they learn to sit ever so still with no hate in their hearts and reach up with their soul to their Creator, we shall be there to comfort them, guide them and give them strength so they may endure everything as a learning and live a life of peace. And so you and we can come together and look at a work well done. And then we truly can all be together and enjoy a perfect time of happiness and bliss."

A Tree

A tree so strong, so full of power
Reaching its branches to the Creator on high
A tree, rustling in the morning sunrise
A tree, shining silver on a luscious green
A golden yellow from afar, to be seen
A tree to be prayed at
A tree to be danced with in sacred celebration
Oh tree, created by the Great Jehovih
To man and beast, a great dedication.

Chapter 3

A Childhood Reminiscence

B ut let us go back to my childhood story. On a sunny afternoon, when I was seated on this wonderful rock in the shade, over-looking the lake and watching with awe the swans floating by, my Etherean Traveller, Ahtmar, said to me, "Let us go back for a moment to your beginning here and take a second look at the day you arrived, because you regard it as if it was something that happens to everyone who walks upon the earth." I remembered so well as his words floated through the soft, warm summer breeze, while he was looking at the flowers. Then he continued, "Do you know that these lovely flowers are to warm and bring joy to the messengers of love, and the messengers of perfect peace? Can you remember that? Could you hand it to people? Could you give it to them so it may change their lives into total bliss? Well, my child, we must again speak once 35

*The
Etherean
Travellers
and the
Magical
Child*

more about this birth, and not drift off into the beauties here upon the earth."

I had gotten up and we had walked for a while when he said, "Come, my child, let us rest here." As we stretched out on the warm, sandy shore of this magnificent lake, he was pointing his finger towards the sky where the sun, a huge golden ball, was just disappearing below the horizon. Yes, that too, for me was a magical event that seems so hard to explain. Yes, I thought, this sunset is symbol of life, of energy, of love and of giving.

He looked at me and said, "You know, we still wonder about the courage you had to return to the earth to give and to reach out to all mankind with love and compassion. Are you prepared, you Magical Child, for the many heartbreaks and the pain that may come into your life? You see, in India they would say that it is your Karma. And in our sphere it is called love for these on earth. We do not see suffering as a punishment, only as a tool for endurance and growth. Now, my child, have you noticed that people react to you differently?" Yes, I nodded, and then recalled that so many of them behaved so different toward me.

And Ahtmar said, "Often people feel or sense the frequencies of whomever is magical and has been sent down to the earth, or, in your case, has chosen to come down. Some try to lash out because they translate this frequency into being very wealthy, others into a feeling of power, which they feel they need to attack. They do not understand that that feeling of power comes from you. As a result, they conjure up false ideas. They may want to suppress the power they sense coming from you and may even have outbursts of anger. But you will know, and you will be able to guide them. For that is part of your mission, to help them grow. Are you prepared, you Magical Child, as you grow up on this earth and learn to walk with all of mankind? Are you really prepared well enough to handle all that is coming, all that will be happening to you? Later, when you will be discouraged and in pain, will you remember the time we sat here on this wonderful beach? Will you remember the soft and silent gliding of the birds that flew by and the myriad of colours and the rustling of the trees? Will you remember about compassion and love when the day comes to move everyone out of your life? Will you remember, my child, that only those who are temporarily physical have been removed and not your companions from the heavens? Neither will I ever be removed, for I shall come often to give you comfort and enlighten you and the work you do on earth. I shall help and guide you."

And then he touched my hand gently and, with his wonderful mystical smile, said to me, "You will be strong, yes, you will be strong when the hour of your mission comes, when you have really learned to understand that. When you have really learned to have insight into their lives, into the ways they act. Then, my little child, then you will be ready for your mission and to start journeying upon the earth. You will be ready once more to surrender all which will have become so dear to you. There will be information that only you know how to use and that is there for the moment, as you need it. You know that by surrendering you become free and more powerful. Remember the courage you need to have in order to fulfil those things we have sent you to fulfil."

I looked upon him, realising the many hours of confusion and the many hours of intense pain I had experienced, and remembering the various people who have travelled through my life and who I didn't understand. But also the many times that I was proud to be such a child. In many ways, I was like the child out of whose hands you could take the candy and who would not stop you in your greediness and who would forever keep loving you.

Little did I know that, many a time, that was exactly what would happen—whether they were earthly items or whether it was something from the Etherean Worlds that they tried to take. Sometimes it was a very lonely journey, but other times it was full of laughter seeing how people reasoned and thought or acted out, not thinking of what the outcome would be.

Time moved forward and it was quite peaceful for a while. Ahtmar, my Etherean Traveller, came and went many times and we had little chitchats. Then, one day he said that he would manifest in a different form. "Do not be afraid, little child, when there is a war or

The
Etherean
Travellers
and the
Magical
Child

when other things are happening. We will always be there to protect you. We love you and we are always close and near. Please try to convey this to all the people here upon the earth. We are continually the Guardians—everybody's Guardians. Those who love and care will be less fearful and also will live a more peaceful and enjoyable life." Suddenly he got up, saying that he had to hurry Home, and left. Was it the upcoming thunderstorm? Maybe. I was left there sitting, pondering about the discourses we have had, however brief.

At another time, Alika, my Ethereal Friend, was talking to me of something else that is very important to be handed down to all of you, so why don't you come closer and listen to what I have to share. He was talking of those who went into transition. And what's so great about transition is that afterwards you can travel Home. The word transition, not death, was used. For you, who so many times use the word *death*, I say, "No, no, no." Should I become like you and question? No, I can't. I definitely cannot. For upon this earthly path and this earthly living I get to receive such beautiful, joyful evidence of the continuim of life and such magical gifts from the Heavens. And the Great God of Light who is manifesting these gifts for me will also be very pleased for I am handing them and the magic to you. Magic? Oh yes, of course, magic! I understand again why I was called the Magical Child. There is so much magic if you only open your heart and continue your Spiritual growth and keep on your path.

Are you rested? Give me this wonderful magical smile, you people, as I sit here and radiate my love, my Light and my healing to you. Let me wish you peace and a journey of great understanding. If you are a person who is in balance, or an aware person who has learned all about the mysteries, energies, power and empowerment, you might be able to understand what I have to tell you now. For those amongst you with less awareness, let me take you on this 'possibility tour' of Everlasting Life—on a 'reality tour' of being able to create what you can envision. Now listen to Alika and what he taught me to teach you.

Imagine that you went into transition and you wanted to appear somewhere, but not as a physical being. You could appear as a magi-

cal balloon. Or, maybe instead, as this great ball of light. Wow! Just like the sun! That is how you can appear. You can appear as a ball that glows of soft golden light. You, at that moment, become the ball of light, for that is what you decided to become. You, the ball, can then decide to speak with those you love and left behind. You know that if you appeared all aglow in the body, in some countries they would have you shot, but to appear as a precious beautiful ball glowing in the room, would not be as frightening. This is the power to transform from material to etheric light.

Let us imagine now. "Imagine?" you say. Well yes, you see it is by will that you can decide to be a physical body, a beautiful golden ball, a flower or a tree. What is it you would decide to become? You can become whatever feels comfortable to you. You have a choice what you would like to appear as. And whatever you decide let it be a decision of truth within your heart— a truth of knowing and a truth of understanding. Yes, I know there are many people doing research trying to change energy or trying to create a new life. They have not gotten very far as yet. Be pure in soul and have power.

Are you comfortable here? Are you peaceful? Yes you are. Now let us imagine that we do some exercises of trying to balance the energies in your body. Okay, sit very still and stretch your legs. Stretch them out. Now gently lay your body down. Do everything gently, not suddenly. Gently, for these frequencies are very fine and powerful. Gently. Okay, you are lying down with your arms next to your body, palms down towards the ground. Oh, what a feeling! Smell the fragrance of the fresh grass! Smell the earth in the warm sunshine. Feel how you are one with the Universe. Okay, now pull your legs up, feet on the ground and try to put your hands on top of your knees. Have you got your hands on your knees? Yes, that's fine. Now stay like this for a couple of minutes. Be still. Be totally still and rest there. Do you feel the peace? Now what I would like you to do is count to seven very, very slowly. As you count to seven, I want you to take in a very, very deep breath. Wonderful! Excellent! And now sit up into the lotus position. Can you do that? Of course you can! Again, put your hands upon your knees. Close your eyes and breathe deeply and slowly. Count to seven breathing in, and count to seven breathing out.

39

*The
Etherean
Travellers
and the
Magical
Child*

"Why are we doing this?" you ask. First, we will repair the passages of energy that are the Cosmic meridians. Then we are going to see if we can adjust your electromagnetic field so that once more it becomes powerful. You question the energy lines that run through each and everyone's body which are part of your electromagnetic field? You may have heard people speak of Applied Kinesiology which works on the body's electromagnetic fields! There is power, energy flowing through your body. Your heart pumps, and some people say that it is just a big muscle. Well, that is their idea. The heart is like a generator that pumps the fluid around in the body, just like an electrical generator outside that uses the water from lakes and oceans to create electricity. Your body is made very similarly. Your lungs take in the oxygen, the kidneys filter out impurities. The liver, that metabolic powerhouse, keeps the body's chemistry in balance. And the heart pumps and pumps, but why is it pumping? It could pump even if you were not there.

"What did you say?" you ask. "It would pump even if I were not there?" Yes. You can lay your body down and you can go upon a journey. You see, what's ultimately left of you is the Spirit, the Soul. You still maintain the brain, whether in or out of the body. If you left the body, you would still be attached to it by a long silver cord which allows you to travel anywhere throughout the Universe.

Now lie upon the ground again, palms down. Train yourself to think peaceful, loving thoughts as you are now learning to breathe rhythmically. Count to seven breathing in, and count to seven breathing out. Count slowly. Once you have learned to do that, we shall go forward on the journey for you will have an adequate supply of oxygen and energy. The more oxygen you have, the further you can travel. The cleaner the air, the more powerful the love and the energy and, of course, the more power there is for you, the soul, the Spirit, that part of the Spirit within your body. Exciting? Yes, you bet it is exciting! Now, do you understand? Yes, you do! Well, carefully I shall explain to you all the magic, the magic of what was explained to me by my beautiful, wonderful friend, Alika, who came to me from the Etherean Worlds down to earth to share as much information as was of use to anyone who is ready, willing and able to change or to adjust or to accept. Sometimes we cannot readily accept a change. It takes a while, and the Etherean Worlds know that, because we have been reprogrammed again and again by religions or by various dogmas that are out there in the world, and by whoever controls them. They sometimes try to wipe away that which is reality but they cannot do this for reality is you, the soul who is all love and all knowing.

And James rematerialized and said, "If you want to be brought back to your senses, back to the realization of who you are and what you are made of, look at the lovely message that is within the Tree of Life high upon the top where the beautiful branches are reaching out to the Heavens, just like a springboard up to the Etherean World. No, no, not all is lost. All was lost before. Because you continued on the wrong branch, you had to turn around and go back to the trunk of the tree in order to be able to climb higher and higher. Now you may stray here and there. Sometimes it could be main branches, but they would never, ever lead you back to the Etherean World of understanding your Spiritual Self. However, now that you are upon the tree and you are aware of your journey, new things will happen that will purify your thinking, your direction."

At one time I asked the Etherean Traveller what would happen with mankind if they could not find their way back. And Mr James looked at me, smiled and said, "Of course, child, they all can find their way back, no matter where they are or who they are. When you go upon the Indian Reserve, you will see that your ancestors had built sweat lodges near the trees. They would go in and pray and cry to the Great Spirit. They would come to self-understanding. Life would become renewed and all-powerful. This is your answer. There are always ways back to become calm, loving and healing, so everything is in balance again."

Mr James said, "Now remember also that when you walk upon this earth, fear is the most destructive power. Greed is another that will throw you out of balance. So does jealousy, which begets hate. You see, jealousy comes from greed. I want you to reflect on what you can do to get to the top of the Tree of Life. It doesn't matter what you

*The
Etherean
Travellers
and the
Magical
Child*

did before. Sometimes you find yourself in the centre of a change and you do not understand what is happening. Now, my child, you must pardon me, for it is high time in the Universe to analyse the Tree of Life, to find the pinnacle, the magical part that will give you strength and empowerment, peace, harmony and happiness. Remember, the greater the pain, the greater will be the happiness. The greater the misery, the greater will be the joy. Everything is within your reach. You are the one that needs to change, not anybody else, as we pointed out already. Remember this as we journey with our Etherean Friends. Now that you understand the Tree of Life and how to reach the top, it will appear less confusing to you when we are saying that the more you give glory to the so-called 'flesh obsessions,' such as sex and as with food, or being rich with material things, and hoarding money or whatever, the more they gain control over you. Some may be obsessed with the body and with sex. Of course, the further you drift away from your Etherean Path, from your Etherean empowerment, the more you lose your Spirituality. Yes, the more time you spend in anger or being critical, the less time you spend preparing for your Etherean Journey homeward to your Resurrection.

"Well now, we have come to the understanding we need. Let us now discuss frequencies and vibrations. I am going to explain to you that when you come to self-realisation, you will recognise that you are made out of all kinds of frequencies, lights, colours, minerals, etc. And you consist of all kinds of energies. Whatever is found at the four corners of the earth, you will find within you. Now, let us take a stroll along the ocean. Look, the palm trees are waving in the wind. The sun is glistening upon the water. Look at the beautiful colour the water has. Isn't it blue? No, the water is not really blue; it is only the colour of the sky being reflected. Are we not all reflections of God, the Creative Power in the Universe? Ah, you are looking at me with great wonderment, my child, as we are giving you more knowledge that will get you back in balance, return you to a state of joy and happiness, and add to your growth and Spiritual Enhancement."

And Mr James smiled and said, "Let me take you by the hand and let us stroll over to that lovely gentle semi-shaded place where we shall sit under the trees. What are you seeing there? Elves? Did you not believe that Elves existed? Did you think that they were only in children's stories? Isn't everything just energy? Are you and I not made out of energy? How many journeys must one make to come to this absolute realisation? Look and smell the ocean! What a lovely breeze of tropical flowers it carries. Link up with the smell. Do you like it? Of course you like it. You are so quiet as you look at me. I shall explain to you, my little friend, all those great and wonderful things, all the magic of the Etherean Worlds."

So Mr James, my Etherean Friend said, "As we continue upon our journey, we can sit on the ocean shore, we can go to tropical lands, or we can stay here, with you in your bed and me standing beside it. Try to reach your sense of being human. For this moment we are using an earth brain to store the information that later you can pass on to the people who are seeking spiritual growth and are desirous to seek their journey Home.

"Now let us find out what energies are. You take a tuning fork and you make a sound; that sound is an energy. You sit in front of a piano and touch the keys. You get high, medium and low tones which are light, medium and warm energies. The white keys are light energy and the dark keys are warm energy. We cannot say dark energy, for it does not exist. Warm energies, yes, my child. That is what it is all about—warm energies.

"As I am standing here, I am vibrating into a materialisation so that I become visible to you. However, as you know, at other times I am vibrating only into semi-materialisation. I can also come in an audio state so that you can hear me. Much later, mankind will start to comprehend what I am telling you today. They believe they know everything about the Universe and the Etherean Worlds. But you know that their memory banks have shut out the great understanding. Therefore, my child, as we move forward and upward, we must look upon everything as it is and at the same time try to bring mankind along with us.

"You must not allow them to call themselves Gods. They are Gods in the making, for a God not completed is not a God, is it? You

The
Etherean
Travellers
and the
Magical
Child

can ask them: 'Can you create a tree for me? Can you create an ocean or a mountain that I can see?' Of course they can't do that. They are only in the making, only in the process of learning to create.

"Now you know that there are vibrations and energies. Within energies and vibrations are colours. 'Colours?' you ask. Oh yes, indeed, colours. Let me explain to you what colours do for mankind and why there are so many upon the earth. Colours are vibrations and frequencies and, as such, every colour has a different tone.

"Remember, we just spoke about your piano having different sounds. I can explain some more to you. Within your spine, each vertebra has a different sound, a different tone and also a different colour frequency. Listen carefully and you will come to understand that you have plenty of Spiritual tones within your spine. Most people do not realise that the little vertebraes of a dog—yes—also have different tones, different sounds and different meanings.

"And then you have meridians, which are spread over your entire body. You say you never heard about meridians? If you buy a violin, do you not look if it is built well, how the strings are and what sound it makes? It is the same with the Etherean Worlds. You come upon the earth and start off, maybe, as a mineral. 'Like a mineral'? you ask. Yes. Because the Heavenly energy that you prefer to call the Great Spirit, the God-like energy, is in the minerals. The minerals have been created by that same energy.

"Let me explain. You see, you live in a mineral world—the earth. Minerals are also in the stones and the rocks, called the bones of the earth, the foundations which buildings are built with and stand upon. Yes, there are also minerals in the sand on what sometimes looks like a muddy road, threading through the forest. There are the trees that grow within the earth. There is also your body. You see, after you will have left the body on this earth and you have come Home to the Etherean Worlds, that body will disintegrate and mingle once more with the earth. However, let's continue assessing everything that we want others to experience as well, as we are now journeying through your learning experience.

"Then, from a mineral, you might decide to become a rock, a

flower, a blade of grass, a tree, or whatever. Your light evolves more and more, and there comes a time in the Etherean Worlds when you might choose to go down to the earth to become a person—a physical being who walks upon the earth—a being who later, much later, will evolve and go from Spirit to Angel. Oh, but now we are running ahead of our discussion.

"When you are growing older, you will be hearing all about meridians because we have been busy for a long time to convey to mankind all about them. An understanding about the meridians of the body would bring them closer to the magical understanding about who they are.

"Now I have told you the story about the Tree of Life. Actually, it is not so much a story as it is reality."

But let us go forward on this journey to learn more and more about what my Etherean Friend has taught me.

Chapter 4

A Life Everlasting

Some people have questioned as to why it was that I, this Magical Child, had such a very hard childhood. Why was there so much heartbreak and discord? Well, had there not been that much imbalance or had the cup not had a bitter taste, I might not have had any interest in listening to the teachings or in seeking comfort from my Etherean Friends. I would be tired at night from all the playing and the very physical challenges, but also from much enjoyment, with so much to think about. However, if life is painful, one is not inclined to concern oneself with all that's miserable, re-running it in one's mind. One tends to shut it out. No, it was not a time of make-believe! Of all the information that I received from my Etherean Friends during their many journeys to the earth, every single fact that has come from the Etherean Worlds has now been proven by science, medicine

The
Etherean
Travellers
and the
Magical
Child

and by people who have had some absolutely wonderful experiences.

You see, I am only attempting to help you in the way that the Etherean Travellers have helped me. I am trying to help all of you on your journey to have a greater understanding as to where you came from and to whence you will return. I do not say to you that you have to accept this as gospel truth. Who knows, maybe in the years to come, you will go back in your mind to this moment and realise that yes, there *are* some people upon the earth who are so enormously privileged to journey with these Etherean Travellers.

My friend, Ahtmar, has now returned to continue his teaching. Sometimes his moment is a little longer than this fleeting-by flash of energy. I asked him how he was going to explain to the many that they really were not in the Etherean Worlds since they truly believe they were. (This refers to people who have had a life-after-death experience.) They believe that they had arrived in the Heaven of Heavens. Of course, with the number of theologies, all those who have been 'there' for a fleeting moment thought that the atonement of the 'there' was such that they had found the place they would want to be at forever and forever.

Ahtmar said, "They do not understand that there are many realms beyond what they experienced. That is where the problems develop upon the earth. They are not ready to hear that this is only the first state of paradise and that it is not the ultimate place. However, if we took that away from them, they would have to come to the realisation that it is only like the playing out of an illusion. They would then feel as if we had robbed them of something that is absolutely perfect. This is the plane (dimension) so many mediums speak of—the plane where the houses, the beautiful lawns and the communications go on. No, no, my dearest Magical Child, I am not saying there is no such a dimension. Of course there is.

"Let us think about all the wonderful experiences they could encounter if they could only be made aware that there are seven plateaus. Maybe we can find a way to get the message across to everyone so that they may go beyond and upward to blend with the Light on the ninth level into the Third Resurrection, the final place where

Jehovih lives and the Angels reside."

Alika arrives to give his perception of the life of the Magical Child since 1966. He explains, "Let us now look at the Magical Child. Since 1966, she had been living in Canada and decided to journey back to Rotterdam in 1971 with her children. Her custodial sister and some other family members greeted them at the train station and the sister could not help mentioning: 'You know, it is strange, but you were never really one of us yet you look exactly like the custodial mother. You were always so different from the rest of us. Do you know who you really are? Do you want me to tell you what happened before you were born and at your birth? Do you know anything about that? And when my mama passed away you were barely three-and-a-half years old.' (You notice she did not say *our* mama.) The Magical Child smiled and answered that she had a few questions herself.

"Later, the Magical Child related to them the story as it is told at the beginning of the book. Then the conversation turned to the veil, or cowl, she had been born with, and to the lady who had received it and was supposed to be the child's Godmother—Cora or Dora Dillon. The Magical Child had stayed with her in Den Haag for a short time after her custodial mother's death since her father considered her a nuisance, and also because she uttered statement that put him out of balance, and even frightened him. What he did not realise was that what she said to him would later help him grow spiritually.

"Her sister continued to tell the Magical Child more of the events that occurred at the time of her birth. 'You know, the doctors thought that there were Angels present in the room during your birth.' How would they know about such things? They were medical men. I do not know. The sister continued by telling of the many thing she was told this child was supposedly meant to do for the earth and that, at an older age, after having received all kinds of training from the Etherean Worlds, she would lead mankind back up onto a Spiritual Path, for that was her purpose of coming. That she would go onto a mission of love and direction for all mankind, giving them guidance and strength. Then, once more, mankind would return to a realm of peace and understanding. And some of you have already, as

The
Etherean
Travellers
and the
Magical
Child

shown by the stories of children who have gone into transition, or by elderly people whom I have watched doing it. Do you want to keep on thinking that this is due to the lack of oxygen in the brain, as might have happened to those who have had surgery and were poorly hooked up to oxygen and recounted similar stories of leaving the body and returning? Some of you want to believe that these experiences are caused by the effects of drugs which create hallucinogenic effects by a chemical reaction in the brain. Fine, if you want to believe this. But listen to the rest of the story and see if this would not really give you the evidence of all that is out there for you who can see, and also for you who cannot see, clairvoyantly. But maybe your psychic sense will now increase because we shall surely help you to do that.

"Imagine, for a moment, that you could see yourself clairvoyantly reading this book. Well, then you are not really reading the book, are you? You are reading that which is reality, and may become your reality. Let us take a look at this. Why would the Etherean Worlds send someone who was totally different to experience the earth's miseries as well as its joys? Wouldn't it be so that this person could experience mankind at its worst with all the pain and the suffering that so many of you go through each and every day?

"Let's look at this from another angle. If you really were spiritual—all of you, I mean, not just a few—wouldn't it be so that you would no longer need police? Do you know that, on the first plane after the earth, there are prisons, hospitals, lawyers, etc.—everything you find here on earth—because the learning goes on? But there is also the other place where it is beautiful, glorious and wonderful, where everything is so good and peaceful. And then there is a plane where some of you will travel through in order to do your thinking, and you get a glimpse of it. This is a place that is not quite so pleasant—the place called Hada which is called Hell to some of you. And the valleys where those go who have gone into transition and who do not understand that they should sojourn to the place where their loved ones are, they stay entrapped in the earth plane until the angel workers come to assist them. But for those whose lives were evil and out of balance, they would stay entrapped in Hada.

"You know that you have choices to make in life to arrive at a state of total loveliness, kindness, peace, beauty, harmony, etc. What shall we call it? Shall we call it being just? 'Being just, what does he mean by that?' you ask. You know what I mean. Just means being honest, kind, respectful and loving to other people. You know, all the greed, the money, all the anger and hate hasn't gotten people anywhere. It has only brought more confusion, more hurt, more murders, more anger and more theft to the world. Isn't it time to experience the changes within and around you?

"Now, you might hesitate here for a moment if you were not always just thinking that it is a very fearful concept. The first impulse from some of you may be: 'Garbage, put the book down, don't want to hear about it.' From others: 'I cannot change, I cannot turn around and make it undone! It is sort of frightening what I am doing to myself.' Then again there are the others of you: 'I don't want to be reminded of how it should be, or how it is, or how it could be. Oh no, I keep my life living right the way it is.'

"Well maybe, just maybe, we should sit down and find out if this is such a wise idea. Are you ready? For instance, we have the second-hand car dealer who knows that a particular car is mechanically inadequate. Here comes a man with not much money who is struggling to feed his family and to survive. The dealer swiftly comes out of his office saying that he has just the right car for the man, although deep inside he knows that this car will not last taking the man back and forth to work. Does the dealer care? No, of course not, as long as he sells the car and makes money! What is going to happen to him in the future? Did you ever hear, 'What goes around comes around.' I hope that you have thought about this. So let us find out what is going to happen next. When the car dealer comes into the other world to the first plane, he is put into a position where he must carry the consequences of selling a bad car to this poor man. What do you think would happen with you?

"Mr Scrooge fits right in here, you know. Charles Dickens was definitely inspired by the Spirit world when he wrote the story *The Christmas Carol*. However, the title is misleading for this is a story

The
Etherean
Travellers
and the
Magical
Child

that should be told more often than just at Christmas. Here we have the banker to whom this poor man, who is struggling financially, comes for a loan. If he could get it, he would move forward and do better. However, the banker decides not to give him one because he has no assets, although he might be trustworthy and a lovely person. And there are others. Yes, there are so many of you who want to sell something that is very, very poor, or do a job that is very shoddy. Well, you know the words, 'Do unto others as you would have them do unto you.' These words replay themselves through every part of your life. If you came to understand that these words were really a gift from the higher realms, you would change your thinking. However, this is my opinion and needn't necessarily be yours.

"Let us go to other situations. Imagine that there are people in government, for example judges and lawyers, with a similar attitude. Many who do not have money are ending up in prison or other terrible situations because of people like that. We have also some of the prison guards abusing the women who are incarcerated. What do you think will happen to all these people? And then we have some medical doctors who cannot keep their hands off their patients! You do not want to think about these situations? I want to make you think because it is time that you travel with the Magical Child and learn to see the reality.

"Do you proclaim yourself Christian? You do! Are you enjoying this book? You are? Let's look at the following for a moment. It says in your scriptures that if you are a looker, and you look at the wrong thing, pluck out your eye. If you steal that which does not belong to you, cut off you hand. If you do something evil with your foot, cut off your foot. Did all of you Christians do that when you were unkind, dishonest, mean-spirited, etc? I can hear some of you! You run to your priest or to someone else to tell them what you did. Did this help you to become a better human being? Did it bring you to a point of change in your life? Or did it just make it easier to continue to be what you are, to continue with what you were doing? I can hear you thinking, 'This Etherean Traveller is tearing open our consciousness. Is he accusing us." No, I am not accusing any of you. I am making you see who you really are. Were you cruel? Were you withholding the child from your husband/wife who was going to visit? Do you know that the child in later years will suffer and will feel the pain? The child will have thoughts that go back to you that might not be so lovely.

"Some of the Angels who are with you are working on their own trials and tribulations at the same time as they are guiding you and giving you the right direction. If you would only follow their advice you would not need any police, for you would be policing yourselves. Why do you think that the world is in so much pain and suffering? Why is there so much crime among the young people? Why is there so much upheaval and so much imbalance among so many of you? Some of the young people are resentful of their parents and will not listen to what is right. They will neither accept discipline nor loving advice. There are those who are rebellious and feel that even at age 12 or 14 they know better. Some of the business owners, parents, who are working very hard to bring up their children, have them stealing out of their till or making off with items from the store when they were not looking. And the youngsters thought nobody would find out!

"Let us take a look at other societies. For instance, some of the Halderman and the Hutterites who live in colonies go to town to sell the tarps off their trucks, just to get spending money. Others in the colony have more access to money, more abilities to have material possessions because they happen to belong to the family of the bosses. The result is bitterness that arises between the colony members. The ones who sold the tarp may think that they are clever when they come back and tell that someone stole the tarp, that it blew off the truck or even that it just disappeared. Did it just disappear? Did it blow off the truck? Ah, you see, the soul knows what happened to it.

"Then we have the person who works in a garage and whose brother needs a tire or a battery. One day the tire or the battery disappears from the inventory. This is why the owner of the business is having a hard time to pay the rent, his employees, and his expenses. The owner may be worrying late at night as to how to make ends

*The
Etherean
Travellers
and the
Magical
Child*

meet. Unfortunately there are so many other examples.

"And then we look at the other side of life. There is the person sitting on the street corner, totally disillusioned or broken inside for whatever reasons that were so painful. Many people like this just cannot seem to be able to get up to fend for themselves. What are you saying: 'Welfare bums?' Not necessarily. Maybe they are souls that are in serious pain and a loving word, a kind hand or a little uplifting would just get them going. Sometimes it means to spend some time to assist them so they can find some work or some means to help themselves survive. Then we have those who are too old. They worked all their lives very hard, but, for one reason or another, never had the opportunity to save for themselves. Now they are living in great poverty and suffering. It could be the neighbour next door. She was left with a bunch of children, will not receive assistance and has to struggle just to survive. The very limited income is not enough. Then there is the couple who lost their business and they are having a very hard time, and are so confused. There is also the person who is sick.

"You know them all, I hear you say, but you do not want to hear more about it. You could become one of them, by circumstances beyond your control. 'Me?' you say, 'that couldn't happen to me. I have hundreds of thousands of dollars; I could never become one of them.' Yes, it can happen to anyone.

"Let us blend back once more into the Magical Child's story. It was right after the war. Everyone was celebrating. Soon it would be carnival time and the people were so delighted to be relieved of the stress, the fear and the worries of the war. During the war, as we know, the Etherean Travellers came to protect the Magical Child, making sure that her immediate family would survive also, for the child would eventually end up under the guidance of the Etherean Travellers in different places. This would later cause great concern for this family.

"However, at the time, they felt great relief. All the members of the household were Roman Catholic and this carnival was an enormous feast they were looking forward to attending. It seems that the Magical Child was constantly either a liability or in the way. In this case, a decision was made that they would all go to the carnival as soon as the child was asleep, including the father, just for a short while to see the late-evening parade go by. Since it was quite cold, they had an electric heater plugged in in the study. The child was in her room sound asleep. They also owned a young German Shepherd dog that was left behind with her and was becoming restless. He began to play with the jacket that was hanging over a chair near the electric heater. The chair tipped over, right on top of the electrical heater, and the jacket caught fire. The fire spread, filling the house with thick smoke. There was clothing, carpeting, books etc, all bursting into flames. One of the Etherean Travellers touched the child, saying, 'Wake up! Come with me!' The child, however, was almost in a state of suffocation due to the heavy smoke everywhere. 'Hurry, hurry, and bring your little canary,' he told her. The Magical Child looked up, frightened and unsettled as she was urged out of the door to quickly go to the neighbours. When they saw the fire, they hurried over to the burning house and put out the fire.

"By now the child had survived several life-threatening illnesses and happenings, one after the other. At age three, for example, it was tuberculosis, and at age four-and-a-half, it was dysentery. It seemed that she would catch just about any illness that was among the population. She was becoming more and more fragile as time went on.

"Time was progressing on and everybody was reorganizing their lives. The Magical Child was about to experience her first summer since the end of the war. As it would turn out, this summer would be a very dangerous time for her. One day, when the child went with some people down to the beach, she fell into one of the mine holes in the water that had remained from the war. These holes were not visible at high tide, and the child would have drowned had not someone from the Etherean Worlds once more come down and made sure that she was found. The Spirit of the child had again been forced to go back into the body.

"And then there was another incident. As every summer, the fair grounds, with all the happy sounds, the smells and the music of the organ, were in full swing. The air was filled with children's laughter.

The
Etherean
Travellers
and the
Magical
Child

The Magical Child looked longingly through the window, watching the attractions, but she was not allowed to join for fear that something might happen to her. Oh! Wouldn't it be lovely! Look at all these other children having a good time. However, one person in the household took pity on her, gave her some money and made her promise to return immediately so that no one would know. She darted forward and jumped and skipped towards an attraction that had little boats. Now, this Magical Child was dyslexic and poorly co-ordinated and therefore needed more time to climb into one of the boats. While she was still trying to get in, the attendant, not realising this, released the lever. All the boats lurched forward, and the Magical Child slipped and fell into the water. Again, the child was out of the body as she was now lying under the boats in her fluffy pink dress, looking straight up. Then she moved upwards and, standing there, was looking on like all the others as her body was recovered by the attendant who had stopped the boats.

"I am telling this in the hope that grieving parents may take solace in knowing that, although a child's adventure on this earth might have been only brief, his/her happy Spirit stays with you for a while before going on towards further Spiritual growth and the learning process. There is no pain or fear—just love.

"To continue with my story, the Magical Child was happy and content, dancing behind the lifeless body. She danced and danced and had a good time. Why were they so upset as they carried the body swiftly to her residence? When the body was laid upon the table I made a very stern remark to the Magical Child: 'Go back in there; you belong in that body. No, no, you are not coming Home with me. You need to get in there.' Soon enough, the Magical Child found herself within the body again and everyone around her was filled with joy and excitement to see alive what they thought was a lifeless body. But the Magical Child felt trapped and limited again, also sad, lost and alone because I, after giving an encouraging smile, faded off the scene. You see, so many of you are wondering about your life here upon earth. I can promise you, there is everlasting life, life after 'death.' Again, I would like to stress this upon your consciousness, but it is your subconsciousness most likely to remind your soul that you are a perfect Spirit—a spirit from the Great God of Light. You are a person created by Jehovih and descended from a wondrous place on high—a person to have a journey here upon earth, a journey that must be fulfilled, a lesson that must be learned by the physical experience.

"Let me tell you why. You are upon the earth to learn to love, to learn unconditional love. You are upon the earth to create. That which you create, you create daily. Many times you wonder about prosperity. What is prosperity to you? What is poverty to you? What are riches? We have talked about it before but I would now like you to ponder some more about it. For when you hear the solution, you will understand. Well, prosperity is having a sense of well-being, good health, and having a sound mind. Most of all, your greatest riches are having caring people around you and you caring for them. Remember, there are many forks in the road that you travel.

"Then there is health. Health is something you need in order to feel happy, to be in a state of contentment and of constant learning. Those are the things that are most important, especially unconditional love. Can you love unconditionally—loving without return? I want you to remember that you are here on a journey through life, a journey to have friends, to share, to grow and to be all-powerful in your knowledge. That is why you are here.

"On with the story. Summers came and summers went. This is now the spring when the Magical Child was to turn nine. She still had a very hard time with the housekeeper who showed a tremendous amount of anger towards her and would take every opportunity to scold or severely punish her. She just could not get to understand this child. The child, again, was not well at all. Although she had been taken to various doctors and hospitals, it seemed that there was no help for her. Was this because the child had such a yearning to go Home and was hoping that she could put an end to this earthly journey? It certainly seemed that way, as we watched what happened next.

"When the child's health became worse, the father took her to a very good specialist who had been recommended. This specialist said that major surgery was needed and that they must hurry, for he did

The
Etherean
Travellers
and the
Magical
Child

not know if there was enough time. Surgery was performed on the right leg and another incision was needed in the right side of her abdomen. The child came out of the surgery and the surgeon thought that everything was under control. Wonderful! But no, the child just wouldn't heal. When it was discovered that the infection had travelled from the right side to the left, they decided to do more surgery. The child came out of the operating room on a stretcher, a nurse took a look and declared that this child was not going to make it. Then she was lifted onto the bed.

"This time, the child went on her own journey Home very quickly. She had not really awakened from that which they had given her as an anaesthetic. There was a slight feeling of heaviness in the body and then she was out of it, moving to the upper corner of the room from where she left. Out, up and away she was speeding, and the city became smaller and smaller as she went higher and higher through the clouds. Then, as if something had triggered an engine, her speed increased tremendously. She passed by something which looked like a beautiful place, and suddenly there was a decrease in energy and she landed on this soft, luscious lawn. Looking around, recognizing the place, she thought, 'I am Home. I have come Home and I am going to stay Home. My Home, beautiful Home with great big round pillars made out of marble with pink and lavender colours, shining in the afternoon sun.' As the front door was wide open, she really felt she had arrived back Home. She moved forward to approach it.

"Right then I, Alika, appeared and started to speak, 'What are you doing here?' She was still standing there looking around with a great feeling of joy and marvel at this so-magical place. The sounds of the fine crystal atmosphere were so gentle and joyous. The singing of the birds—nothing like the earth ones—so heavenly was the chorus. It created in her heart a feeling, a greater yearning to stay Home. As she was looking and watched the others gliding by in deep telepathic conversations, so peaceful, her heart leaped up from joy. No one on earth in their wildest imaginations can imagine even this heavenly glow. The stillness, the peacefullness, one must return to feel harmonious.

'Oh yes, oh yes,' she said, I am really staying Home.

"And then I asked, 'You know that you are to be down there?' She looked up and said, 'No, no, I am not going back down there. I am staying right here for I am Home now. It must have been fulfilled what I was to do down there. No, no I am not going back down for I am really Home now.' I waved my hand, parting the grass to form a great circle. I instructed her to look down through the circle, to see through the roof of the hospital and to watch what was going on. She looked and saw a flurry of activity around her lifeless body.

"I then instructed her to look more closely. 'There is your papa. You must go back to him, this man needs you.' But she repeated, 'I do not want to go back there, I want to stay Home. It is so beautiful here—lakes with majestic swans, flowers more beautiful than any colours on earth, strong, healthy trees with birds in them that had the sweetest songs, and happy were people floating through the atmosphere and communicating telepathically.'

"Listen to what I promise you" I said. "I promise you that if you will go back down, when the time is for you to return Home, we all will come to bring you back. I promise you this.

"After discussing this some more I told her that she must go now. The time was late. And I took my hand out of my sleeve and gave her a gentle but firm push. With enormous speed she went down to earth and her Spirit landed back in the body upon the bed, giving a loud scream as it did. The nurses looked up in surprise and shock because she had been gone for one hour and 45 minutes. They realised they had just seen the impossible for the body had already cooled down too much to all of a sudden come and bring itself back to life."

● ● ● ● ●

A biblical story comes to mind here—the Good Samaritan. Remember that story? Isn't it sad that we have to be left with a story like this. Wouldn't it be better for us deep inside to realise that we should rather be the Samaritan than those who pass by and say, "I'm not helping," or "It's too dangerous," or "I'm not getting involved," or "You've got to be kidding, I have to have my money." Is it really your money? Is it not Universal money? It is most important that you get to understand how it works in the Heavens. You say, "But this is

*The
Etherean
Travellers
and the
Magical
Child*

earth and we are here. We need to work hard to make money and to control everything we can possibly control. After all, money is the most important thing in our lives."

Money takes you away from your Spirituality, as does preoccupation with sex. What else? What else are you hunting for in the material world? Yes, those things will take you away further and further from understanding and listening to the Spirit. There are many people out there who proclaim themselves to be the new world people, but in reality are as materialistic as you. The Etherean Worlds are not pointing fingers at anyone. Definitely not. However, they are wanting you to assess the way you are living here on earth and what is most important to you who are spending time together here on earth.

You might know neighbours who have gone to one of these countries where there is so much hardship and you think they are a little "out to lunch" to have brought back a child to adopt. Or perhaps they went there helping with the relief effort to decrease the pain and suffering. I don't think that they are so far off track. Maybe they are in tune with their Spirit Guides and are working off some of the things that need to be worked off on this earth.

Do you not think that there are earth changes coming? Well, we shall ask the other Etherean Travellers what the guidelines are for each and every one. Oh, I hear you. You are reminding me that we were going to teach you how to attain greater Spirituality. Yes! Of course we shall. But first, take a few minutes to analyse what is within you, what is most important to you at this moment. You need to do that before reading on to what the Magical Child really has to tell you. "Yes," you say, "I hear you speaking now, you Magical Child. You have already offered that to us, but you haven't gotten to it yet."

No, but must you not first analyse what your life is all about? What have you done to others? What have you done to yourself? What have you allowed to happen to yourself by the unkindness of others? Open the pages of your Akashic Records and read all the pages. You are saying that you want to change, but you do not know how? Yes, we shall help you. Remember, we promised that the

Etherean Traveller will assist you in becoming more loving, more kind, more uplifted and more attuned with the new world that is coming. We shall also help you to become attuned to the Angel world, and they will come into your life.

So, my dearest friend, why don't you take out pen and paper and write your name on top. Write out everything in the past that was painful, everything that really hurt you. It might take you a day to do this, but I want you to do it now. Do not put this off until tomorrow. You might need several pages. Also, include everything you did to someone that was painful, mean or unkind. You do not want to do that? You do want to become Spiritual, don't you? We promised you that there would be a lot of healing happening to you—healing on a large scale within you. Well, then, write down the names of all the people you will truly forgive and, on another sheet, list all the deeds done for which you will have to ask forgiveness. You do not have to visit people personally, but you will have to ask for forgiveness. That is easily done as you continually tune yourself in by saying, "I forgive . . ." and name them one by one until you are through the list. Also, do not forget to forgive yourself in the process.

To ask for forgiveness, you put your right hand over your heart and you say, "I promise myself and the Angel world to love and to set myself free that I shall be open, loving, kind and in tune, working together with the Angels for a better world. It does not mean that I shall never express the emotion of anger again because this anger would consume me. But I shall heal. I shall heal within myself and I shall help heal all those whom I have hurt or who have hurt me. When I have set everybody free, I shall be able to declare that I, too, am free at last."

You have done it? Isn't this better now? Did you have a good cry? Did you feel emotionally quite out of balance? Yes, that might have happened, but that was of your own choosing. You chose to heal, you filled the pages and you assessed where your life is at today. Tomorrow we shall hear some more from an Etherean Traveller. I bless you. I bless you and shall pray for you all, that you may find peace, harmony and joy in your life.

The
Etherean
Travellers
and the
Magical
Child

When I Die

Angels, angels when I die,
I come soar with you on high,
I come wander,
And play in fields,
When new moon comes high in the sky,
Then, my precious angels,
You will take me back on high.

When that hour comes of your sojourning to the First Resurrection, look for those of the Etherean Worlds, and the Angels who will guide you. Do not be fooled by those of Hada who come to lead you to their dark place. And do not linger near your body because physical life cannot be regained, and attaching yourself to your relations and loved ones can keep you earthbound.

Chapter 5

A Spiritual Journey

Shall we continue with the spiritual lessons to achieve further spiritual growth? Are you ready for the Etherean Traveller again? Yes? That's good. Alika says that if you want to stay in balance and if you want to come into perfect harmony, it is a good idea to eat a lovely fruit in the morning after getting up. In the winter, to eat fruits of every colour—the full spectrum, if possible. Dried prunes will do for blue and purple. Blueberries kept in the freezer would be a good idea for all year round. They are good for the growth of your soul, for this is part of your purification.

You say you want to purify and detoxify yourself? Good idea! Lovely idea! Then why don't you do this. At lunch time, you eat only steamed vegetables, choosing as many colours as possible of those grown above the earth as well as those grown below. Then, at night-

The
Etherean
Travellers
and the
Magical
Child

time, make a big bowl of mixed salad. That will be really good. That is day number one. Day number two is more of the same, plus add a handful of all kinds of nuts, except peanuts, which are not too good for you. Days three through ten are a repeat of day two. How are you feeling after day ten? Are you feeling great? Now don't forget that you also take some multiple vitamins in case you might miss something in your absorption. You now should feel lighter, cleaner and more energetic. You surely can continue this for a little longer, for that is how this Etherean Traveller would like to see that you get body, mind and soul back into balance.

As Ahtmar joins us once again, he says, "Now, we will go further on the journey of the Magical Child. She now had recuperated from the surgery and illness and was getting stronger and stronger, and the Spirit World was also making some interesting decisions. They taught the Magical Child about the new society—the new society that would come in the future. The child asked, 'How far in the future?' The Etherean Traveller explained that it would not be too far in the future. It will be when man starts to feel the vibrations in the Etherean Worlds and starts to speak more and more about Angels coming down to earth, and when he starts to speak about the space travellers who fly through the Universe, and man will also speak about other space travellers and their ships.' The child looked in wonderment at the Etherean Traveller and asked if that's as it was written a long time ago. She also wanted to know about Saint Germain who she had seen in one of her brother's books. Who is Saint Germain? The Etherean Traveller put his hand on her shoulder and told her that Saint Germain was a man who came from the Heavens. 'Just like you, my Magical Child, he came down and wanted to enlighten mankind because he was so advanced in earth thinking—at least, that is what mankind thought. He wrote books about futuristic inventions and changes upon the earth, just as Nostradamus did, only Saint Germain wrote in a little different manner. Now you know, little child, it will be quite a while before this will all be known to mankind. But there will be books found at the right time to enlighten mankind about the major changes that will take place upon the earth.' He asked the child if she knew what was going to happen upon the earth?

The child looked back at him with great wondering eyes and said, 'You know it is a sad state that, even in my case, people were told that I was coming, but were expecting this to be the role of a male. Why do the Etherean Worlds make it so hard on me?'

Ahtmar replied, "No price is ever so great as the price of the Etherean Worlds. You see, all of mankind works for money. However, there are a few enlightened ones upon the earth who come and work for Spirituality. If you are selfish and you would be like Buddha, you would call all mankind to you, and not unto the Great Spirit. You would say, 'Come and follow me and you will get to Heaven.' But if you are wise—and you must be wise, my child—you will say, 'Turn within and find within. Perfect yourself within.' It is sort of like a violin upon earth. You could compare the strings with the emotions and the sounds with the frequencies. You tune the frequencies of the soul with meditation and deeds of love and compassion. To abstain from eating that which walks upon the earth or flies within the sky, my child, will make you stronger and stronger. Yes, it is preferable that you also abstain from eating any of the fish that come from the ocean. Then, again, if you did eat of the salmon which goes on its journey upstream and knows that it is going to sacrifice itself at the end of the journey, you would not be participating in the taking of a life. So eating salmon would be permitted at the end of their life's journey. But sardines, for example, are ever so small a life and they should not be taken. No one shall take a life for a life.

"And there are the vegetables and the fruits, which are alive also. The fruit grows upon the tree and falls down to re-seed the earth. It is also there as food for you, just as it is fit for the birds and for the animal world. You can also eat that which grows upon the field. Don't forget to thank it, and to thank the earth because the earth is part of the Universe. Remember how it started from this mineral and then it became something else, and something else again? The ones that have been the longest upon the earth are mostly the trees and the rocks. Yes, those too. The rocks are the bones of the earth, remember? They

*The
Etherean
Travellers
and the
Magical
Child*

are used in the tribal ceremonies.. They go in the sweat lodge. Yes, of course, there are so many things to learn.

"Well, my child," Ahtmar said, "as you keep growing in this physical body, as you will become wiser and wiser, we hope that you will remember everything that we come to teach you so that you can hand it down to mankind and bring them enlightenment."

● ● ● ● ●

I hear people say that some of the thoughts and communications of the Etherean Travellers are Buddhist-oriented. "No, they are Cosmic oriented, is the reply you can give," said the Etherean Traveller, "because you are the being who comes from the Cosmic. You will become wiser to the things of the earth." He smiled his soft, gentle smile, touched my cheek and said, "Remember, compassion and unconditional love to all mankind are the most important things. 'To judge not that ye may not be judged.' This is so important, for you are the one who judges yourself. As you teach others to judge themselves, they too will grow as you will. In a New World, things will be absolutely wonderful and in balance. This is in the making, but first the earth will travel through some turmoil and imbalances."

One day, when we walked along a path in a beautiful garden, he took my hand and said, "Listen and look over there, there is a stream." The stream came dancing down the mountain. It glistened in the sun. I saw that it was so clean and so pure. The sound was like a thousand trinkets of crystal, like a thousand bells in the Universe. He told me that the Spirit within man will flow like this silver stream—a stream of light, of lovely sound. As I sat down, I wished that I could hear it for all of mankind. He replied that they will, they will hear it if they sit still for a moment. That is the answer—the very important answer— to be still. To be still and find God, the Creator. Be still and listen to the Spirit within. Listen to yourself since you are colours, frequencies and vibrations. Have you ever heard of meditation? A meditation is a time of stillness, a time of tranquillity without a beginning or an end.

Become Like a River

The
Etherean
Travellers
and the
Magical
Child

Oh, become like a river,
And flow like the water,
Through God's holy garden.

My dearest friend looked at me once more, saying that he had to go. "I shall see you soon, my Magical Child,' he said, "for we shall take a walk through the Universe and take a look at other places." I thanked him and gave him a quick smile. He very softly became a cloud. I whispered goodbye and sent my thoughts of love. I felt lonely and a little lost. Once more the journey amongst mankind was a hard one.

I was not understood. Never mind not to be understood, I did not understand people either. They did not understand kindness and thought it was something to be used to obtain something material from others.

Today I am still often told, "You are too giving, you are far too kind." I am asked how I can love people who are cruel and mean to me. I am asked why I pray for them. Shouldn't we all? As I told you, we all shall meet again. Perhaps there will be a hundred, a thousand or even five thousand years in between, but we all shall meet again. We are all particles of the Light. When we reach that point of Oneness and of understanding the frequencies of the Universe, we shall all blend with the Light. I pray for the blending, for the day of total bliss and total joy. At that point, we shall all be part of the Universal Mind that creates all good and all life. We shall be joined with those who love and are all good. That is what my Etherean Friends told me and so I am telling you as we are going back to the story of the Magical Child.

• • • • •

Of course you must understand that continually the Etherean Beings have come and gone and taught me, and encouraged me to bring peace and harmony, and to keep the thinking or thought-form

The
Etherean
Travellers
and the
Magical
Child

in balance. But where I was living, it was not very easy to stay in balance. There was a lot of child abuse, pain and suffering. Yet, when I am asked today if I am angry, remorseful and bitter, there only comes a lovely smile and the answer is, "Oh no, why should I feel this way?" We shall eventually meet again, and maybe, in the meantime, as I journey upon the earth, they will learn right from wrong. They will also get to understand that they came to the earth just to learn to be compassionate and loving. What's important to understand is to treat little children very lovingly because if you beat them, lie to them or you deceive them, these acts will have severe ramifications in their later years. Part of this impact is that some of these children will mould themselves after these adults and later become cold and rude in behaviour. Others may go on to become thieves or murderers, and those who are confused become batterers themselves. They will become people who are lost, whose Spirituality has left them. We realise that the elder acts according to how he/she was handled as a child. Do you think that a child under one year of age does not learn? He/she learns with enormous speed!

This does not only apply to the elders, but also to those with positions in institutions of learning—our teachers. It also applies to others in positions of authority such as policemen, or the officers of the courts. It doesn't matter who they are. They are failing the Creator for they have gone astray. Yes, they go into professions that are supposedly caring and gentle, but in reality they do it for the money and not because of the kindness and the good they could accomplish. Would kindness and loving enlighten them? Would it strengthen them? Of course it would, but they do not think about this.

My Etherean Friend has often pointed out how important it is for a parent to have Spirituality, especially between the first month and the seventh year of the child. Parents and caregivers need to be continually loving and help with the enlightenment of the child to understand his/her path here upon earth. Many families do not realise that each and every household is like a nucleus, like a cell. It is like a small world, in fact.

To follow the idea of Spirituality, let us look at people who have been suppressed for centuries. It matters not what country, or what part of the world. They had to do everything they could just to survive. The Spiritual ones would have found ways to survive and to be strong. Those who were less spiritual would have resorted to different means of survival—survival that might have caused hardship to someone else. They had become bitter. They looked at their fellow man, whether of the same race or not, thinking that they had it better, that they had more, but that actually they themselves deserved better and to have more. And sometimes it was true that they did have more earlier on. Now they had lost their Spirituality and became totally hardened, bitter and jealous of others. They would look at things out there in the world that they thought they were deprived of. When you came into the world you were totally naked, as was your father and your mother, and everybody around you also. When you pass away, remember, you go out and leave the earth, sometimes in a white gown, sometimes in a suit, sometimes in whatever, but, in reality, you are leaving the earth totally naked. Isn't it important to realise that you come with nothing and you leave with nothing?

At least, leave with your empowerment and with your Spirituality intact, and with your mind clear, peaceful and harmonious. Isn't that more important than all the riches you can own? I ask you this: there are so many houses, businesses, things and money that you own upon the earth—can you take it with you? Is it going to buy you Spirituality, peace, rest or harmony? What is it going to do? To whom are you are going to leave it? Can you imagine that they will fight over it? There may be a great amount of anger and jealousy generated by what you leave. If you have no relatives, to whom are you going to leave it so it can be there for someone in time of need? Sometimes it is a temporary joy when you have left it to agencies or whomever. What is it doing in so many instances? If it went back to the government, are they going to bury you? No, of course not. It is important to be buried in peace and dignity. The body came upon the earth, it travelled, it worked and it learned upon earth, and after its journey you want to lay it to rest, for you are finished using the physical body and you are ready to go Home.

Chapter 6

Even in Winter there is Holiness

I, Kiryon, now come to continue with the journey of the Magical Child at age 12. By now, she had become quite industrious in helping the survival of the household. It was after the war and the father had lost all his earthly wealth, partially due to the war and partially due to the divorce from his second wife, a German lady. They were very poor and the hardship was enormous, but they were peaceful. To keep the household going and since he was very good at photography, he would go and take pictures of people. There were many people in those days that wanted to have photographs of their families, especially the people who lived upon farms. The Magical Child had gotten her first motor-driven bicycle and, one early morning, some photographs needed to be delivered to these families. In order to save paying someone, the father thought it a good idea to have the Magical

Child deliver them. She would return long before dusk. Off she went travelling along country roads, delivered the photographs, then turned around to go home. On the way back, a tremendous blizzard developed. It got very, very cold with no shelter in sight and the little motor quit. As a result, she had to push her bicycle. It became dark and she was cold and tired. Ice had formed on her little jacket, her feet were extremely cold, and everything was either sopping wet or frozen stiff. Then she noticed a small shed on the side of the road and thought it was a good idea to take shelter under the overhang of the roof.

As she proceeded to sit down, holding her little hand on the handle bar, another journey started for her. Sophia, from the Etherean Worlds, came and asked her why she was sitting there. She answered that she was so tired and cold. Sophia told her that she would warm her, but that she must then immediately get up and be on her way. She closed her eyes and it became really nice and warm. It was very comfortable, but now it was the comfort of hypothermia. She started to shiver and then she found herself outside the body looking at it slumped over, with the bicycle leaning against her and the snow blowing in on top of her. We do not know how long she sat there before the Etherean Being materialized and waved down a vegetable delivery truck. The driver stopped, looked over at the heap on the ground and exclaimed, "Oh my, I know who this child is. I know who she belongs to." Quickly, he lifted the child and the bicycle into the truck, and when he looked back at the person who had stopped him, he could not see anyone. He was very sad because he thought that the child had now gone to the other side. However, as the body began to warm up, she opened her eyes and declared that she had not left. She told the driver that she had seen every move he had made, that she had seen all the traffic going by. "My Etherean Friend did not allow me to return Home," she said, and explained how she had been talking with her Etherean Friend about many things and how important it is for people to love one another and to have compassion. Yes, compassion without schemes about what you are going to get out of it. Just being kind and loving is so important. Why is it that often those who really did not suffer in their life have so little compassion? You see, they

The
Etherean
Travellers
and the
Magical
Child

didn't taste of the bitter cup. They didn't experience the taste of suffering. That is why it is so difficult for our Etherean Friends to touch them and to get them to understand that learning to love is the foremost journey in a person's life.

If someone gets continually rebuked while they are small, they learn to be listless. They go to school and cannot concentrate, or be focused on that which they should be focused on—their Spirituality and their learning, so that they may have a secure future. Many times parents do not understand that the encouraging words they say will be encouragements for a lifetime. Similarly, when you use negative words, they can continue to stay with a person causing low self-esteem for a lifetime. This is what's so important. You do not want to victimize children, do you? If the Etherean Worlds have given you the opportunity to facilitate this lovely, beautiful soul in your life you must remember how gentle and fragile children need to be handled. Yes, they are so fragile. Their minds are being formed and their Spirituality is there for them to remember where they came from. However, every time they are being bruised emotionally or physically, their soul is being bruised. They get programmed with negativity upon the earth. This is so important for teachers in the schools to realise that, by being so kind and gentle, you raise a kind and gentle race. Yes, a new tomorrow with loving people, loving children, would be an absolutely perfect and harmonious place.

Back to this Magical Child who had long learned to understand that there was the continuance of Etherean Travellers coming from the Etherean Worlds for people's support, strength, harmony and their learning. They are coming from the Etherean Worlds in droves every new moon to help those who are confused. They also come down to support those who have just passed into transition, to lift them up and guide them towards the Light. They guide them not only to the Light, but also to many other wonderful places. For many of you, this will be so difficult to understand. Isn't it much easier to imagine that there would be places in the Etherean Worlds that are similar to earth? Then, for you to make the transition from the earth to the Etherean Worlds would not be such a hard and difficult process.

*The
Etherean
Travellers
and the
Magical
Child*

Remember, the Etherean Worlds are filled with love, compassion and kindness towards you. Everyone upon the earth is facilitated by their love and their Light. Accept it and learn from within not to be judgmental, not to be unkind. It doesn't matter who they are or where they came from; eventually you will all blend together with the same magnificent Light. Not only will you blend together, but imagine for a moment that you have come to this time in the Universe, when you have learned and you have passed through all the planes of the Etherean Worlds. You will hear from the Angels and the Guides about this marvellous Light. There is the opportunity for you to work continuously towards total perfection—total peace and harmony within yourself. Your Spirituality will be the highest pinnacle. No, you are not losing your mind, even when you are blending with the Light. You are becoming the perfect empowerment within this Light.

Someone asks, "You say that you constantly return to the Light?" Yes, I would like you to really think about yourself and the blending with the Light, for eventually, when that hour comes, you will remember how important it is. When you are upon the earth and you journey through life, so many times when something appears to be negative, you can instead find something there of great value and of great learning purpose. "Great learning purpose?" you ask, "out of negativity?"

Yes, nothing on the earth is negative, or in the Universe. Everything is both—positive and negative. Remember, sometimes you wear these little pendants around your neck or you see these signs on packages that say yin and yang, up and down, light and dark, shiny and dull, heaven and earth. Those are all forms of yin and yang, of having both poles of the magnet present in the one article. They are like the North Pole and the South Pole on the earth, which are positive and negative. And then you have hot and cold.

So, for example, perhaps you went on a trip but never reached your destination because something may have happened along the way that made you stop. You would have declared, "Oh no, I didn't want this to happen, I don't have time to spend around here." And maybe someone came on the scene from whom you learned something absolutely magical and of great value. At that moment, it might not have seemed that way but when that person left and you went on your journey, either on to your destination or back home, you suddenly remembered that out of so negative an experience, transpired something really good.

Then you ask: "How can there be good in the situation of the Magical Child when she had it so bad? When she was found frozen at the side of the road, what was good about that?"

Well, here it comes. For the man who stopped and lifted her into his truck, it meant soul growth. It meant realization and understanding. He also had a learning experience about Spirit because he really thought he had seen someone at the side of the road waving him to stop, before he saw the child. Once he saw the child, there wasn't anybody there. For the Magical Child, what good was it to her? She had a chance to speak with the Etherean Traveller and to learn more from her. To learn that, no matter what circumstances and no matter what time or space you are in, there is always someone to love you, someone to guide you and to be with you.

I am certain that you can recall many incidences in your own life. Look at them and see what you may learn from them. They may have been the darkest times in your life, but you have learned wonderful things—whether it was compassion, being more spiritual, or being more attuned to the Universe. You see, there are many ways of learning, many ways to come to understand that no journey upon earth is without experience that can be used tomorrow.

The Etherean Traveller said to the child, "Man puts so much stock in money, what happens when there is no money? When there is no money, there is no food, no shelter and then no survival." "Oh, wait a minute, there are social agencies," you say. Yes, but do those social agencies really help people? Are they really reaching out to the people in need? Isn't it instead a means to supply more work, more jobs for social workers? You see, if they took these suffering and confused people and helped them to learn a trade, to teach them a dignified way of survival, it would be of greater advantage than making them dependent on social assistance for the rest of their lives. But the agencies keep control of these people by never giving them enough to

*The
Etherean
Travellers
and the
Magical
Child*

be able to grow and develop and become independent. This control, being the one handing out the money, gives some civil servants sitting behind the desk a feeling of power. What about the one sitting in front of the desk? What is going to happen to that person? That one wants to move forward too, and wants to feel secure and know that everything is all right. But because they do not get enough money from this hand-out, some are going to scheme. This set-up is making them dishonest. However, they are merely seeking survival.

You see, we have children in Brazil who go scrounging in the garbage dumps where some of these so empowered people come with their rifles to shoot at them. The ones who survive this ordeal become hardened, their Spirituality shrivels up. In some cases, there is still compassion for one another and they form gangs. Within the gang, hatred and bitterness towards those who have becomes the norm. This is a preventable situation. However, there are no laws in the land to protect little children, to lift them up and make them strong. In Brazil, they shoot children, don't they?

The Etherean Worlds, therefore, are now urging you people here upon earth to become aware of these goings-on, to become aware of war. Did you know that when children who have been caught in the middle of warfare, many years later, after they are fully grown, perhaps in their 30s, 40s or even their 60s, may cringe with fear and look for cover when they hear the sound of a tire blowing out? Hearing any other sudden, unusual noise, they will look as if they want to hide, for the insecurity, the pain and the suffering are still all too real.

You see, more than ever, the earth has to come to a point of change, a point of understanding. You may be learning through this book and the journey of the Magical Child how life can be filled with many trials, tribulations and sufferings. Even though, for the Magical Child, there was also an enormous amount of emotional and physical abuse, she survived. Didn't that alone make this child magical? On this earth, there is much abuse happening to so many children, even when people live in fortunate circumstances. We experience so much waste and so little compassion for little children who suffer. We also have the people who suffered so much while striving and struggling through many years of hardship earlier in their lives and who are now trying to live out their lives. Then we have a younger generation who is slightly embittered, who feel that the old ones do not resolve anything. Remember today, the yesterday, and also think today of your tomorrows. Your tomorrow might be that you suffer somewhere as an old senior citizen in some place barely being taken care of, or under some care where they drug you up even though your mind is still alert and fine. It is very seldom that the mind comes to a point where it no longer functions. But sometimes the connection between the mind and the body is the problem.

Chapter 7

Maturing Life

And further you are travelling through the life of the Magical Child who is now becoming older, twenty-six to be correct, and to have intact the connection with the Etherean Worlds is even more important. She had gotten married and was having her own children in this world. The marriage was a very bad situation. Often, life situations arise which people are not able to understand and which some call 'karma.' This Magical Child understood about dark forces that would stop a person on his/her journey of growth and learning to give, believing that they can stop the Light from flowing and from growing brighter and brighter. Moving forward is impossible if these forces interfere with a person, but there can be help in times of darkness that will give enlightenment, an enlightening guidance to all mankind. Therefore, let's look at the wisdom of this

The
Etherean
Travellers
and the
Magical
Child

Magical Child as she progresses closer and closer to the Etherean Worlds.

We are now looking at the time period of 1964. On one particular occasion, when the Etherean Guide, Mr James, was visiting again, he made her aware that her life was moving forward rapidly, and that she should realise that even though she had children in her life, the journey she was being prepared for was going to happen regardless of whether or not she understood. He invited the Magical Child to go on a journey with him to the absolutely incredible atmosphorea. Before that, however, he was going to teach her something of great value and of great interest.

Before we start this lesson, I want to tell you a short story about how the Angels saved a life—the life of the only daughter of the Magical Child that entered into this world. She had been born in a private clinic in Genoa, Italy, with a serious need for a blood transfusion, but there was no one to be found with the correct blood type.

The doctors were ready to declare that she was too far-gone and that the RH antibodies had done too much damage. There was a Hungarian friend of the Magical Child, named Horvad, who had studied medicine before he had left Hungary, and who offered to try to help. He phoned around and came back saying that Professor Sansone knows about blood more than anyone else. When the professor came to see the daughter, he gave her mother, the Magical Child, a long look and said, "I know that you are a Magical Child. I am spiritual too. I know that you knew what was happening. Why did you not make sure that they would listen?" The Magical Child looked at him and answered, "I tried to but they didn't understand." "They knew that you were different from the rest," he said, "because I remember them speaking about it." She looked at him helplessly as he continued, "It is now between you and your Angels if she lives." With that, the Magical Child picked up her baby, looked up to the ceiling with great despair and asked, "My dearest Father who art in Heaven, can you hear the conversation? Did you hear that they say there is no hope? You told me that this child would be born, and now I put all my faith and love in you, for this is a great testing in my life."

The
Etherean
Travellers
and the
Magical
Child

After the doctors had tried for many days to save her life but nothing was working, the Etherean Traveller appeared to the Magical Child and said, "Why don't you ask them to boil some carrots, cool the hot water that comes form the carrots to room temperature and give it to the child, and the child will be well." When she turned around and repeated this to the pediatricians and Professor Sansone, the latter said, "Maybe she is right, why don't we do what she asks. After all, we have given up." The Etherean Traveller followed them as they were preparing the carrot water and, as they gave it to the child, this wonderful, magical Being held his hand over her chest and spoke to her. A smile came upon the baby's face and true colour returned to her cheeks.

Thus, this RH-factor condition which had gone too far for the doctors to control, turned around and earthly life was restored, just as it was decreed by Jehovih. Still, today, the Magical Child remembers this great gift of life and she humbles herself and gives thanks for the great and wondrous world provided by Jehovih.

As life travelled onward, the Magical Child moved to Canada. She thought that now maybe the troubles would be less. Little did she know that, as it was coming closer towards the year that the Etherean Travellers would gain control and she would be considered under their mastery, she would be ready to go out amongst the masses, to speak to them and give them this message of eternal change. You who are Spiritual will enjoy this message, but you who are not will criticise it, take it apart, put it aside and call it rubbish. Sooner or later, the Angels will come knocking on your door and ask you if you are ready. You will have to give your own answer. The prayers of the Magical Child are that your answer may be positive and that many blessings, peace and harmony will fill your heart. Angels are real, you know; they really exist.

It was about 7 pm one evening when the Etherean Traveller came back and invited the Magical Child on a journey into the Etherean Worlds. "Come, let's go for a stroll. Let's go and see that which you need to know and record so you may later be able to speak

The
Etherean
Travellers
and the
Magical
Child

about it. It is high time for people's Spirituality to come first and that they recognise that which is good and wonderful in the Universe. Many people down below have 'out-of-body experiences,' possibly through sudden 'death' (that's what they call it). But is there really a death, an ending, a finishing? No, there is no death."

There is that period when we have the Angelic Beings standing by to help those souls which are returning to the earth to inspire all mankind. "Does everyone return to the earth?; does everyone reincarnate?" you ask. No, no, not everyone. There are a certain few out of the masses who return but do not reincarnate. Instead, they receive a body that was already prepared for them because the soul will not pass through a birth canal twice. The Creator creates the soul only once. So these are the ones who return continually to the earth to guide and to raise man's spirituality. They come to the earth as messengers, as teachers, to guide whomever needs the Great Spirit's love. I hear your next question: "What about suicide?" Those who commit suicide are received in the Etherean Worlds with great love and compassion, but also with a stern warning that this is not a way to gain control. This is a way to have your journey prolonged. Negotiations, discussions and healings go on so that that person later chooses to return to the First Resurrection to accomplish that which had been decided to begin with.

I believe that those amongst you who are mystical and have that empowerment will immediately recognise one another. For those amongst you who are not yet at that place where you can see, feel and hear manifestations of Spirit, it is difficult to understand. No, we are not always perfect, but we surely try, and many a times, because of our journey, the earthly plane and the earthly way of dealing with people can set us in confusion. It is true that not all the time do I understand what motivates those who are on the earthly plane, or what things they conjure up or the games they play. What guides me is that I continually listen to those from the Etherean Worlds who are there most of the time.

Here, I would like to remind certain people of the things they did, but we will discuss that in the next book where you can read

about some of the horrendous situations I found myself in. "Why did-
n't they protect you?" you ask. But they did. They tried desperately.
You see, it can prove very difficult to walk with one leg in one plane
and the other in the plane called earth. Many a time, we do not understand, we really do not understand why people do the things they do.
What is the prestige that is so important you have to gain or what is
it that you are covering up? What is your ego? What is your anger? I
pray continually for those who have caused me great pain. I also pray
for those who have now gone on to the First or Second Resurrection
or 'below' and I would like to send my love to all of those who are
progressing onward and upward, overcoming all earthly pain.

*The
Etherean
Travellers
and the
Magical
Child*

Back again with the Etherean Guide, we were travelling through
the different layers until we came to the one that was called Plane of
Awakening. Here we have "fully grown" people who are looking
down to earth, watching and wondering who they shall choose as parents with whom they shall create an earthly life. Some of them have
already made their choice before their parents went to the earth
because they were together once before. Then there are those lovely
beings who walk around and choose the ones that they go down to
the earth with to be able to serve, to help guide. The more Spiritual
and the kinder you are, the more you are in tune and the easier it is
to communicate with your Guides.

"Guides? What are guides?" you ask. Guides are beings who
have been upon the earth and have learned to love, accept what is
happening here and how to live. They also have lived in the Etherean
Worlds for quite a long time and understand to move in the ways of
the Etherean Worlds. They come down by choice and guide other
beings.

"How does channelling work?" you ask. Well, many people have
spent a lot of time meditating. Some of them have made great effort
to change their lives to come in touch with the Higher Frequencies.
That's when the Heavenly Beings come close to them and guide them
through the maze of understanding, learning and discipline and, occasionally they also use these people, their brains and their physical
body to come through to speak to you. It is like an attachment, brain

The
Etherean
Travellers
and the
Magical
Child

to brain. That is how that works. People say, "But it isn't a different voice," or "There are still many things that are the same." Yes it would be, because the voice box does not change, usually, though on some occasions it does, depending on if the being living in the body has always been there or if the person is an Etherean Being. If it was an Etherean Being—anyone who comes from the Etherean Worlds— it can make the exchange and make use of the body here upon the red planet.

So now we are wondering about these exchanges. Many times you see people and you say, "She/he was this way yesterday and now she/he is not." Have you known this person for many years? Have you really? If you didn't, you might be dealing with a person who was or who is possessed and gives access to people from the other realm to use the body, although very briefly.

Let's talk about mediums. Here we have different forms. There are people who wait for many years to develop and to be of service to the Spirit World.

"Spirit world?" you ask. Yes, the realm of the Angels, the Guides and the realm of the loved ones who have gone to the other plane. Some mediums serve the Higher Plane, while others are still busy serving the plane where your loved ones are and helping you to understand what is happening. With the establishment of this understanding, communications from that plane become possible. There are other mediums that bring you messages of enlightenment, those who speak about the wonderful other realms. They will speak about the second and the third Higher Planes. You often can see that those ones that come from the Higher Planes are not as interested in giving you messages about your loved ones. It is not that they do not want to, it is just that they are programmed to deal with Spirits from the Higher Realms. They come to raise your consciousness and your understanding. It is really powerful, don't you think, to make major changes in your religious belief, in your religious understanding.? I can hear some of you in the Christian community saying, "Oh, hogwash, don't listen to it. It's all from the devil!"

The devil? Hey, wait a minute now, stop and listen to what we have to tell you! If you are really, truly interested and involved with the man Jesus Christ, didn't he have out-of-body experiences? Did he not travel out of the body and back in at will, at times when it was most necessary? Could that be a scripture that we read? Wasn't he a master clairvoyant? Of course he was. He was a medium of the highest calibre. No, he is not your master! He is your brother. He is the one who wanted to open the door for you for greater understanding. An interesting fact is that he was reaching out to the many religions, the many creeds and races without prejudice.

Let us ponder some more. You see, for so many ages, the earth has covered up, has changed, has adjusted so that man fell more and more under the control of religion and state, with less and less time for Spirituality and spiritual growth.

When we speak of the North American Indian Reserve, many people say, "They are so poor, they are so terribly poor." Are they really? Do they complain about their poverty? They might be very, very wealthy, very rich in Spirituality. That is not to say that there isn't great suffering upon the reserve, especially during the cold winter months. They suffer when their children or their grandchildren come and take their pension cheque and when no one comes to fix the little place they live in. It does not mean that they do not need warmth, love, compassion and caring. They need that too. For those of you who read the book, who are living upon the reserve, Thunderbird Woman admonishes you to let you know that it is time to go back to the old ways and take care of your elders. Also take care of the young ones, for they are the future. Make sure, since they are so fragile, so precious and wonderful, that you raise them up in the knowing of the Great Spirit.

Often, deep within your heart, deep within your mind, you say "Oh, Mataki-ashi-oh," and you hear within yourself that you are opening the door for the path that never will be lost, for no-one to ever go astray, because you are lighting a lamp upon the reserve for the little ones to recognise the way Home, forever. Then these little ones will have great thoughts of love. That is how it works. My Etherean Traveller, Haida, told me that the more love and compassion you send out into the world, the more love will be returned and the better it

*The
Etherean
Travellers
and the
Magical
Child*

will go for you.

There are those of you who are a little bitter. I ask you, why should you be bitter? You see, at one time, it was said that it was more difficult for the rich man to go through the eye of the needle than for the poor man. Well, it isn't necessary to go through the eye of the needle but it surely makes a difference whether you hoard and control your money and suppress others with it to a point that they can hardly make it, or whether you show with love and compassion your ability to help and to reach out to the many in need.

I can hear some of you grunt. Well, many of you have great riches, many of you are really poor. How do you know who is really your friend? Is it because you have all this money, all this power, all these worldly things? But then we look at the other who is kind and loving and has no money but so many friends everywhere. Everybody smiles when they see him or her coming, organizing potlatches for everyone to share.

The greatest concern in the Etherean Worlds is the question as to whether the Indian nations are also following the white man's materialism. Are they following the white man's path of confusion? Isn't it better to walk with those who have one leg in the Etherean Worlds and the other here on earth? For the Indians, it would be much better to keep Spirit oriented to the Etherean Worlds. When things are happening, they will still be aware of Spirit. If money is so much in your consciousness, I feel sorry for you because it will be very, very difficult to hold on and to stay in balance. This goes for all the other aboriginal peoples all over the earth. Do not do as the white people do, do as you were told by your elders and all will be fine. Don't do as they do with their drinking or their drugs. Stay clear, keep your mind centred and keep your heart attuned to the Great Spirit. This is quite a journey that you are making, a journey that was foretold by the elders of old. Those who stayed in attunement, who danced around a tree at the sundance, as you were told, prayed to the Great Spirit for this generation at the medicine wheel. Learn to pray to the Mataki-ashi-oh and bow for the Great Spirit and pray to save the red planet, earth.

Standing Deer suddenly appeared. I asked him, "Oh, Standing Deer, but you have promised us that we would speak about your travels through the Etherean Worlds." "Oh, ho, yes. Mataki-ashi-oh! We shall go back to that path and share it with you right now."

Let us, for instance, look at the journey of birth. As we are travelling through the passages in the Etherean Spheres, we hear them speaking about those who are returning to the earth. You are asking me, "Do those people return to the earth in adult bodies or in the body of a child?" Let me explain how it would look if you could see it with your human eyes. If you could see yourself with your Spiritual Being, you would understand it immediately. Imagine this very magnificent ball. It goes from a beautiful cobalt blue to a silvery haze, to lavender and to a rose colour with a soft fragrance of a rose that doesn't go stale. And, in the centre, vibrating very fast, there you are, part of this light; the 'you' is within it as you come down to earth. Of course, you understand that this being has to go and enter the mother. As it does, it goes into the body and makes the arrangement for conception.

"Arrangement for conception?" you ask. Yes. Of course the scientists think that the body does the arranging of all the cells, etc. The scientists do not understand that there are two forms of Spiritual Beings. There are the ones from the highest of Etherean Worlds and those from the lower planes. Then there are those from the low, low planes also. They also have the same power to play with whatever is in the Universe. It all comes down to free choice. Sometimes there are beings that come from the Etherean Worlds who will also go in your experimental dishes so they may later come to teach you something about the fragile vibrations of the Etherean Worlds. Don't you know that, sometimes, when you are working in your laboratory, you are under the subtle and solemn guidance of the Beings from the Universe? So then, before birth, a being enters the body and makes arrangements. Sometimes it was decided long before coming down whether this person was going to be a boy or a girl. Now, however, being in the body here upon earth, there is time to look around, and come and go from the mother's body. Occasionally, the being discovers that being a little boy would be fun although he had promised to

*The
Etherean
Travellers
and the
Magical
Child*

come down as a girl. Despite the female frequencies that are present based on this decision, a shift occurs and the body is formed as a boy. Thus the body becomes male but there is still within it a strong female soul frequency and we have the confusion at the birth. The troubles begin the minute the child is born and comes to the realisation that he is now in the physical body the Etherean Worlds have created and that he has made a wrong choice. The choice had been made in the Etherean Worlds and should have been maintained. Let us see what you can learn from my journey with the Etherean Traveller.

We talked earlier about animals having a soul. When a puppy is stillborn, there is a beautiful ethereal ball that comes out of the mother and hovers over her abdomen. Within this beautiful ball is the shape of a tiny puppy, all cuddled up. Do you feel that I am giving you too much information? Sometimes after you have disciplined yourself with good deep breathing exercises, as you remain silent, your Spiritual eye will come to be activated. Your Guides can come and work with you so you can learn to see, feel and hear the Spiritual dimensions. Imagine that, after having done this for quite a while, you are sitting in your room with an infrared light being able to see anything you want. I wish that you could see all the wonderful things from the Etherean Worlds so it may give you encouragement upon your journey, no matter how difficult, how painful or how involved with pleasure your life might be. Yes, gentle guidance, not from me but from within yourself, to become a better person, a stronger person and living in total harmony.

Later we shall continue strolling through the Etherean Worlds and bring you back more information that is important for you. You see, your journeys with the Beings from the Etherean Worlds will educate you not to live recklessly here on earth and not to abuse the body that you are in. If you abuse the body, it makes it difficult for the Spirit to live within its shelter.

Chapter 8

An Italian Adventure

And Sophia came and told the story about the Magical Child when she was living in Italy.

In 1964, one day in August, she was strolling towards the church on the Plaza di Santa Margarita. She followed the people who went inside. All of a sudden, there was a strong urging of "Come! Come here!" She went to the door and stepped outside again into the bright light where she saw fruit vendors. Walking around and looking at the produce, she stopped in front of one vendor who had a large variety of all kinds of fresh fruit, trying to decide what she was going to buy. Then, a few steps behind her, a person in bluish-grey clothing appeared, looking somewhat like a monk. He was old and had gentle eyes, and gentle hands were folded over his chest. Looking at him, she was filled with great compassion and turned back to the

89

The
Etherean
Travellers
and the
Magical
Child

fruit vendor to buy some oranges and mandarins which she put in a bag. She walked over to the old monk and handed him the bag, asking him if he also wanted some of the other kinds of fruit. He gave her an absolutely wonderful smile that was quite imposing, and did not answer but just smiled again and thanked her. She walked back to the vendor to buy fruit for herself and, when she turned around again, she found out that he had disappeared. She asked the vendor if he had seen where the Padre, who had just been standing there, had gone to, but he had not seen anybody standing there. She was searching some more for her Etherean Friend, but to no avail. The little market place had only the one door and she looked outside; no, he definitely was not there. The fruit vendor kept looking at her and said, "Let me touch you." When the Magical Child asked why, he replied that he knew something magical had happened in front of his fruit stand that day.

This was just a small encounter, assuring her that all was well and that the Etherean Helpers were always close by and could be as material as was necessary. This encouragement was to last for many years.

As time passes and we analyse the life upon the other planes, I would like to inspire you. I want to reach out to you and would like to bring you to a point of love, enlightenment and understanding of one another. You see, so many of you are unhappy. The unhappiness is created by your own actions of not thinking before you speak or act. Therefore, step back for a moment and analyse your life and how you deal with it. When you hurt someone verbally, do you really feel good or does it leave a feeling of sadness? If you are what is called smart, and you take something from someone, does it really make you feel good? Does it really make you feel empowered? If you hurt someone, what does it really feel like afterwards? I am just checking if you will come to the realisation of your consciousness, of your Spirituality.

As we were wandering on through the higher planes, we are being educated with more information that is now being released to you. I ask you, is this knowledge really a magical or an empowering situation for you as you sit quietly by yourself somewhere upon this earth, or is it something that makes you feel scared and uneasy? Are you scared and uneasy because of the many things that you did that were not right? This is what my friend urges me over and over to ask of you so that you may come on your journey and see that you yourself keep a record of your thoughts and your deeds. Every kind word, every gentle touch, every misdemeanour—you keep a record of it. Still, you are chosen by the Great Spirit, chosen for who you are, to re-make and re-live that which is peaceful, joyful and wonderful.

Isn't it about time that all of you, young and old, are prepared for the journey Home? It is time to prepare for a journey of complete Spirituality and understanding. I did not say religious thumping, only just and intelligent communication with the children about what is right and what is wrong and why one should not be doing the things that distort their Spirituality. Isn't it time to have a better world, a world that is for a thousand years prepared to be peaceful?

You say, "Don't scold us, don't rub it. I want to put down the book and run away from all this." Do you want to run away because you recognise what the soul has to deal with, and it is disturbing you because it brings you to the point of having to look at all of life's options and life's deeds.

Let us find out what else the Etherean Traveller can give to the Magical Child for you. Hold your hand open and the light stream will pour down from the Etherean Worlds just to you. To you, who want to learn, to you, who want to know. I would like you to sit back and close your eyes for a minute. After that, read again the words I give to you. Imagine that you were of a different frequency before and you wandered upon the earth. You chose to be a rock—a beautiful rock upon an ocean shore, or perhaps to be a grain of sand as a part of a beautiful beach. After that, you decided to rise and become a rose. You decided to become a plant covered with flowers so gentle and so sweet that you glorified the Heavens. Looking around, you then chose to become this beautiful little animal, perhaps a squirrel, a cat, a dog or a bird. And then, a choice was made for you to come back to earth just like man. When you had walked upon the earth, great fear fell upon you because you thought that you had progressed beyond, into

*The
Etherean
Travellers
and the
Magical
Child*

the Light. Now, would you walk around in fear that you would be dying? Had you not done that many times before? Yet, once more, you will die as a man to soar high in the Etherean Worlds with Angels and Guides galore. Will you then serve for a time those who walk upon the earth? Will you counsel them in their time of despair? Will you touch and heal them as they sleep? Will you reach out to them to guide them in their Spirituality and it their earthly need?

You chose to soar with blessed Angels, Angels evermore. You offer your Angelhood and once more you must pass upon High. Then, as you leave, your soul can go and you blend with that which no mind upon earth has ever conceived. As you then travel through the Universe, you continually reach out to progress, to understand and experience purification. You will come down to the earth to teach all of man that there are no limits. And you can store your progression and do your relearning here upon earth. You must remember that, when you are in the Etherean Worlds before you come to earth, you have already done a long, long journey of guiding, understanding, healing and comforting those who came back from the earth or those who have gone down. As you learn to understand all these remarkable and mystical happenings, the empowerment finally opens deep within your heart and your realisation of everlasting life then becomes total and complete. Yes, you can progress beyond and beyond and beyond. It is for you to choose to blend, to become one with the Great God of Light—the Great, Great Light that encompasses all of the universe and reaches out to so many travellers who are evolving.

As the Etherean Guide travelled higher and higher with her in the Universe, she asked the Magical Child, "What is it that you see?" "Oh! The world might be reforming," said the child. "Yes, the great, wide earth with all its riches, its living things upon it and the water, the mountains, and all the wonderful, beautiful things that anyone could ever dream of." "What else do you see?" asks the Etherean guide. "Tell me what you see that is there for people to use."

"Diamonds, gold and silver, rubies and emeralds, everything that shines and glitters," replied the Magical Child. "Roses and lilies and daffodils and tulips. Everything that is out there is lovely, is full of colour and has a gentle smell. Oh, all those wonderful things Mataki-ashi-oh, the Great Spirit, has created here upon earth!"

"Don't you see anything more?" asked the Traveller. "Look again." "Yes," she said, "I see the canopy of the firmament of Heaven. In the midst of the firmament of Heaven, I see a light burning." "The light that is burning is the sun," replied the Traveller. "Oh! Is it ever a great splendour!" The Traveller continued, "It is the propeller for the growth of the flowers, the grass and the vegetables and the fruit world." "How magnificent," thought the Magical Child. Then it will be the glory of the day since it reflects the joy of the Maker of Light. That is why the sun was made."

Oh Fire

Oh fire, oh fire, what burns within me
Love of God Jehovih, a God of Fire
Divine is my love, the all
United in one
Living, striving to speak the truth
And uniting the spiritually wise
Living with holy fire all as one
To universal truth
To my holy one.

The Traveller asked again, "Don't you see anything else?" 'Oh yes! The glory of the magnitude,' said the Magical Child. She prayed that man may not forget and may not come to a point of analysing the Etherean Worlds scientifically as if they never really existed. "We spiritual beings must know that He who created the Universe, the Great God of Light, oh Elohim, oh Jehovih, is All," said the Traveller. She stood there in a feeling of absolute wonderment of all the magnificent things that were raised up in the firmament. And what more could we behold? The moon would change from light to dark towards the night watch—the night watch to assist the Angels, the Gods who administer their healing to the mortals and help them into transition.

One side of the world is all light frequency and one side is all

The
Etherean
Travellers
and the
Magical
Child

dark frequency. The Magical Child decided to hold his hand and saw that one hand pointed upwards in the light side and one hand pointed downwards on the dark side. Here lays the brass that wrote on the sacred plate. Above them was the symbol of the burning candle—the symbol of all the prayers of the ancients. Then, above these, low and behold, was the Arc of all the Prophecy.

"Well, my child, why are you stumbling and stuttering in your speech? What is it that you see?" "Oh, my Traveller, above the world I behold an evil fruit that is black and clouded with serpents. Why, above the crossed twin swords, was the sacred name "Oh Elohim, Mataki-ashi-oh. Mataki-ashi-oh to all our people?"

"What do you see in the midst of the tablet and what is it that you can decipher?" asked the Traveller. "Oh, it is a black tablet with a net woven around it," said the Magical Child. "It is a new corporeal world, rich in growing things, sprung from the serpents. There hangs the sacred sign of Holy Laws and our Great God, appointed by the most High, Oh-Elohim, Mataki-ashi-oh, Jehovih, praising and guarding the morning and the evening of the first days. Then the trumpet called below to the earth and the Spirits of the mortals now dead come forth, inspiring teachers in all useful labours to the new world above. A fine, beautiful fabric that is woven in the firmament of Etherean Worlds is descending to the infant called an Iesu, thirsting for a Kingdom in the lower Etherean Worlds going to a new planet not to be seen by scientists."

"Yes," said the Traveller, "for there is a new world being created, a new time. There is also a tyrant who controls the newborn spirits in the lower Etherean Worlds, watching for ever and ever the new earth." Therefore, she asked the Guide if there was a time or an hour when there might be no suffering, no time of worry or fear.

He looked and said, "Only if you can teach people to be totally triumphant and obedient to the Great Spirit, totally abundant in their love and caring for one another. You see, they speak so much about Karma. However, Karma need not be, for there need not be a time of continual relearning, of continually returning to the earth. Do you think that the Great Spirit is a hateful God? Do you think that the

God of Light is angry ? Do you think that the Light of the Great Spirit is not all bright and all compassionate? Do you think that this Light does not come from on High, from the Highest Heavens? Ask this of yourself, and contemplate these things. There need not be a hateful action and an angry action of any kind.

"The earth has travelled through a time with mankind believing in many saviours. Now, once and for all, the time has come that mankind can turn back and they can go within themselves to meet their own God. They can meet their God of Light, love, compassion, peace and harmony. They will not meet an angry God, not a God of hate, just a Light of the Great Spirit to the little Spirit called man, to the little Spirit called 'Angel World.' It is time that you come, my child, to the realisation that is of most importance for mankind, that there is an hour during which all renewal will be taking place. There will be a time when there will be no more hate, no more confusion and no more anger upon earth. Why do you think, my child, that man so are still longing for ancient Saviours—those who once walked upon the earth, bringing God's message of love and compassion? I ask you, child, can you see why they do not make a sacrifice so holy, a sacrifice of compassion in their soul? Peace and harmony, but fighting no more would result. Why not make a sacrifice of abstaining from all that walketh, creepeth and crawleth upon the earth, and that flieth within its sky above the earth and is being eaten? Is it a sacrifice for those who live and those who act upon this earth? I ask you, my child, do you ever, as you sit in your silence, realise what is the greatest sacrifice that you can make? Maybe it could be seen as a sacrifice if you offered your soul, your Spirituality up to the Etherean Worlds, for all peace and harmony for so many others, giving up one's own life and existence upon the earth and the comforts thereof to go amongst mankind and to reach out to them to help them realise that there is a beautiful, magnificent new day coming. Of course, many of them may say, as you may, that I did not need to do this. Oh, didn't I? It is a great warning for all of mankind to call not upon Gurus, Christs, Mohameds, and Budhas alike, for they are not your creators. They will surely not save you. Call out to the

The
Etherean
Travellers
and the
Magical
Child

only creator, the Great Spirit, Jehovih, The God of Light."

•   •   •   •   •

As you are reading this book, are you growing from what is written herein? I surely pray that to my Etherean Travellers my answer can be, yes, I gave you the greatest path of my life. I offered it up to you in service and in payment for the so many kind and wonderful things you have done. This also applies to those I have prayed for so fervently. And if that was a sacrifice, then the gift from the Etherean Worlds was even greater. But I leave it to the Etherean Worlds to analyse what is a sacrifice. I realise that I must give you this one warning that every action you do has a cause and effect. And, out of the cause and effect, if you have chosen the honourable side, then you have come to understand the meaning of the word bliss. I did not realise for many years, but now I comprehend the word and the state of bliss. I can have a state of bliss here or a state of bliss in the Etherean Worlds. The state of bliss is that you automatically have found your way home. Bliss is being homeward bound and, in the Etherean World, to blend with the light, to be a total part of that Light. Bliss is a state that has no beginning and no ending. It just is.

Oh Love to My Creator

Oh love, my Creator,
Now rhythms were created, moulded where the substances then
      formed the summit of the world,
In which holiness was produced in creating worldly gardens, places
      for angels were produced,
So bonding the seen and unseen in a wise will,
A mighty bond was there in all creations,
This line a stream of great glory,
The all wise one stretched his will from on high to all beneath,
A bond not to be severed by any vibrating being,
Who or where did all creations spring,
You who knows, yes truly know.

Chapter 9

An Hour Of Wisdom

I was sitting in the room and thinking about what some of the people had asked me and decided they should have a clear answer. Then a rustling of the paper in the room told me that one of you had landed. The temperature quickly changed and tiny little sparks started to appear. And of course you, my dearest Ahtmar, had arrived with Kiryon. And the two of you, of course, look like a summer breeze, and brought the fragrance of tropical flowers along with you into the room, the warmth and love and the wonderful glow filling the atmosphere. You gave me an answer, my dear Ahtmar, to the very question I had in my mind.

"Yes, my dearest child, my spirit, my magical angel child. Let me then make all of them aware of earthly life. And let me give you some gentle fatherly advice. Let us help you so they will remember. They must always remember that they are spirit first who have become physical and that so many of them have forgotten the ever-so-still and softly-speaking voice, the voice that will warn them of danger, a voice that says or makes them feel watch out or makes them feel uneasy. Or worse, you or they become immobilised because the guardian power is so strong. And then, when you have not listened to the small gentle voice or the feeling, then you know you are not safe. And for you, when you are so aware of great danger, do tell them. Do not allow them to discourage you with their forever-material excuses and their creations of why they could not when the very warning is sometimes endangering you to give them opportunity for life."

"Be careful when you advise them. If they need to give money to those in serious need, to tell them that they are not giving away their power by giving assistance and by giving love to those who need it so much at that moment." And then, I, the Magical Child asked, "Power? You ask me, power?" "Yes. Material things are considered power. Money is considered a tool of power. Some of them believe that they are better than others. Those are the ones who must learn the most. Remember they only realise that they are physical first and think that they are spirit last. Never did they ask was the egg there first or the chicken. Of course, the spirit from the Great Spirit of the chicken was first. So teach them that first impressions are very powerful and do not second-guess. Teach them to listen to their so-called premonitions—the warnings of their Angel Guides." And they waved two guides closer. Kiryon and Ahtmar spoke to the two who had newly arrived and were going on to a post of a freshly born child, to teach the child a time of forgetfulness. And Kiryon said, "So fresh, so precious to come from a love on high to experience the red planet." And I said, "I sometimes feel great sorry for the pain in the beginning for the new soul endured. How could one so easily forget one's heavenly home?"

And they wished me a warm goodbye. I also said my goodbyes.

Chapter 10

Universal Discussion

As Haida and I were walking, we were speaking about the map we were working on, and I was speaking to him about the solar system. Then he said to me, "Hey, I will tell you some things about the solar system. Bye the way, did you ever get an answer on spontaneous combustion?" "Wow," I said. "Is it only jumping from the stellar divider down to the physical body down here on earth?" "Oh yeah", I said, "whatever is of interest comes first." "No," he said, "you had that question about the combustion, how it took place in the human body." "That's right," I said. "I noticed a short while ago some of the so-called smart scientists could not figure it out whether it was true or whether it was murder. Of course, you and I know it was true. Spontaneous combustion does exist."

He said, "Well, we'll have to go back to the sun in order to

The
Etherean
Travellers
and the
Magical
Child

explain to them spontaneous combustion." "So you do," I said. He said, "No, no, the vortexian needles that point from the sun... Oh, oh, let's go back to ancient times when they knew and they called the sun Tow/Sang energy. And they knew in those days, and it was more visible then, than it is today, because of your high pollution levels. Also today, even though not totally understood by mankind and definitely not the scientists, these inhabited corporeal worlds have their existing vortices and similar conditions as your red planet earth. Saturn has a life form like here. Mars has had, and still has, some life form as here. Jupiter and Mercury are the same and have corporeal energy. These are, of course, the ones that are visible from earth with peoples' and scientists' telescopes. Then there is the planet Zarandanderoz, the lovely green planet, where everything functions on telepathic communication, where it is gentle and flowerful. This one they will know about by the year 2002, but will not be able to sojourn there with their technology. But some of the sweet inhabitants from there have sojourned often to your planet and voiced major concerns about your disrespect and disregard for all the others in the universe.

"Destructive mankind is polluting the solar system with debris. From the planet Mars, have come many of the space sojourners to the earth and like, to warn the earth that many of those have moved to Saturn and Jupiter because of their own destructive behaviours—a progression of greed. More buildings to take away the green colours of these planets have led to the planet Mars, its destruction. The planet earth is out on the same journey. Remember that the Great Spirit said everything I created and create has life form of one kind or another. The very universe you are in is life. The air you breathe, remember, is life.

"So back to the energy we go. So the sun, as you now know, was created with many needles that create and reflect light. The needles are pointed to the centre of the sun, which then in return create atomic force, which then becomes a sensation of great heat. So that is the law of the Great God of Light's creation. It manifests fortexian energies found also in seeds. So when man partakes to consume many grains and seeds and then eats very ripe or over-ripe fruit, then espe-

100

cially he comes in great danger because he is creating within himself a nitrogeneous condition. As he then eats nitrogeneous plants, so called nightshade, or those who like to be grown in the dark. For so as he then partakes of breathing exercises after the consumption of these edibles, the edibles then go to a state of desolation. And the gasses are built up in man. They become dislodged in the body and we have an inner atomic explosion, which is called spontaneous combustion." And so we looked at each other and we smiled. And he said, "Isn't it funny? They created a rocket-controlled 'going home'." And we smiled and said this was a wonderful dissertation. We hope the scientists will enjoy our explanation. We gave each other an embrace and smiled, for nothing material is everlasting.

Become Like an Eagle

Become like an eagle,
And soar through the sky on high,
Greeting all heavenly beings,
Who come so nigh.

Chapter 11

An Hour Of Meditation

As I was sitting still one night waiting for the people in my meditation group to arrive, Sophia, as beautiful as ever, came dancing in and showed me her latest creation. Her long, long hair had now many colours and her dress flowed in the wind. And she landed on the floor right before me. "Hey, hey," she said, "Ahtmar is coming. Isn't it wonderful, we together here?" I inquired, "Where are Mr. James and Haida?" With her wonderful smile, she informed me, "Oh yeah, they are on the way. Clear night you know. No thunderstorms to be nervous about." As I responded, "Are you really nervous about thunderstorms?" "Yeah", she said, "I don't like the great electromagnetic fields to be disturbed as I descend and pass over the red planet. The others are not as touchy about it as I am."

And I look up, and she looked with her head slightly tilted at

The
Etherean
Travellers
and the
Magical
Child

me and said, "Hey, hey, they are soon coming, the people who come to you." I nodded my head and said to her, "You promised me a while ago that all of you were going to come and chant here." "Yes," she said, "we shall do that tonight." And as she spoke the last word, the others from the Etherean Worlds had arrived. And all greeted quickly with a nod of recognition and then proceeded into our telepathic (Tele) chant. So we shall share the chant with you. For you who do many meditations, it will be of great help."

> Oummmmmmm (7 times)
> Ahhh (3 times)
> Rahamaaa (7 times)
> Ommm (3 times)

"Chant in each and every corner of the room in which you meditate, three times per day. Do this three times in each corner, for 21 days in sequence.

"When you chant the above, do not partake of eating of those created by the Great Spirit that fly in the sky, walk and creep and crawl upon the fields, or those who live within the rivers, lakes and oceans."

And upon this note, the people from my meditation group arrived, greeting one another in love, and started their meditation. Egos were left outside, becoming all one energy so daily they continue to walk in the light. So, and with this, ended the meditation, and they smiled and left into the night.

Over the years, I have conducted meditation classes. I offer to you the following meditation attunement as a guideline in conducting your own meditation.

Meditation Attunement

1. Before each and every meditation, greet your holy place that you have set up with a long O-E-O-IH.

2. Stand in the centre of your room and bow to the four directions (east, south, west, north).

3. Say God's Prayer. Oh Great Spirit, who art in the heaven, Jehovih is your name. Your will in heaven will be done by all so in the universe and here on earth. And so it be.

4. Light seven candles and offer flowers and give thanks for all the good things done for you, and to whoever has had a request to Angel Guides, to Spirit Servers to be brought to the Great God of Light.

5. Chant.

6. Extinguish six candles, leaving one burning.

7. Begin the meditation.

8. Extinguish the last candle when the meditation ends. Leave on a small red light (electric or candle).

9. When you leave your holy place, chant a long O-E-O-IH once again.

Note: Breathing exercises from within the belly are very important, as is sitting straight when meditating. We are recommending groups of 12 sit together to meditate and that they do this on a regular basis, at the same time of day (preferably 7 or 7:30 pm), and with the same group of people. This will build great harmony and give you the opportunity of Angel communication.

Chapter 12

Timeless Contemplations

And now we are speaking with Alika. Alika looked at me and said, "What do you look so sombre for? Isn't it all like a dream?" I looked up at him and said, "Quite some dream they have put themselves into." He said, "What do you mean?" And I said, "The meaning is this. More horrifying and dangerous diseases are returning to this earth." "You're right. What do you want to do about it"? And Alika said, after a pause, "Oh yeah, you're right. We can do something about it", and he answered my thoughts. As I looked up at him with a questioning look, thinking how hard it had been, trying to educate even those who came around into thinking higher thoughts, taking them away from eastern religions. It has been so hard. He said, "Educate them as we have discussed before. Teach them to learn to respect and honour one another, free oneself of anger, and live a life

*The
Etherean
Travellers
and the
Magical
Child*

free of fear. They have been made to believe everything that happens to them happens for a reason. How silly a thought this must be. Haven't they known by now that everything has a cause and effect?" And yes, I nodded, some do understand. He said, "Do they understand and do they practise what they are taught? How often have you reminded them that thoughts are things? They create as they do. How many times evidence is given to them and it feels they did not absorb?" Still, I looked around me and once more looked up at him, "Is there some more we can do?" I asked. "Let us teach then this," Alika said. "So many believe pests and plagues are sent by heaven to your earth. Or they say it came from the Great Spirit. But your plagues really come from Hada. The fallen ones live in these dark places and they must work off their past evil behavior to become good. There are thousands, millions of them and they live in their respective hells. Yes, those who have lived centuries and aeons ago with their terrible diseases, their foulness to bring the pestilence, disease, decay, hatred, terrible poisons, plagues. They come from the low end of the First Resurrection. AIDS is not new in this universe. Tuberculosis, cancer, auto-immune diseases—these things are picked up by humans in bars, sharing drugs, and in hospitals, gatherings in places where people hold Raves, morgues, and angry gatherings. So they hang out and they work to gather and bring more souls to them."

And my face was a picture of dismay. I felt hopeless. I felt so terribly small. As he put his hand on my head, I said to him, "Why aren't they bound?" "Now, now," he said, "You know they were given by the Great God of Light free choice like you and me. You know there are also others who, because of free choice, come from these hells to make progress onward and upwards. When you speak to so many, they listen too—those who live in these hells. It inspires them to progress onward and work more organized. So others, aeons of them, are being enlisted in schools and companies to receive instructions for their progress. And then there are those earthbound spirits who come and listen to your teachings and follow your instruction and progress and grow in desire to be good. They go to the higher planes and go to

school and labour and progress and return to teach here on earth.

They then become the brides and bridegrooms and return to the God Jehovih, the Great God of Light. Then beyond atmosphorea, into the Third Resurrection, these angels work so very, very hard to be whole."

And now I remember Alika is from the third plane. So is Ahtmar. And so I know once more what I am here for—to serve all of you here on earth. I already started to feel lonely again, knowing that Alika was going to return to the Third Resurrection, and I needed to seek strength once more to remain behind and serve Jehovih here on earth. And a great calm came over me. Longingly, I thought, I must work harder so I can one day go home.

Be Like a Cloud

Be like a cloud and flow to heaven,
Before God's holy throne.

Chapter 13

Contemplation for the Self

As I was sitting out late one night on the balcony, gazing over the city, I came to the realisation that now, my dearest friends, the time has come that there is need for you to lay a good foundation and how it will be when you lay a foundation of your own spiritual use. Since the Great God of Light has never, ever created destruction as you then come to the realisation to call out to the self, "Set free, be free, I claim my power now and free myself of the foul-smelling ones." No longer hearing their lamenting cries of torture and pain that pierces one's soul and lingers in the mind. I will free myself and learn to judge myself before the Great God of Light. My first stop would be the gods and lords of the First Judgement and I will pray, find me pure of my past, as I work within my knowingness and clean up my past. Since I know the past stays with me, so I must change

*The
Etherean
Travellers
and the
Magical
Child*

and pray, confuse me not. I pray I will not have to pray or call out that I had not hoarded the so-called treasures, money for my own, not others and their care; that I had not sought to tell the lies and direct-ed it all to you, my Great God of Light; that I did not seek to forget Thee and that my life here on earth was only to serve Thee. This is now what I wished for. Take away all the temptations. Take away all the aggrandisements that I not need to stay before you and cry out these things. I come before you, Great God of Light, and beg you to please receive me. Free me of those who hold me down away from you. Now I have come to know the lords, the Buddhas, the deities, the Mohameds, the Jesus, and the Christs and whatever gods they may be, and they are not the Great Spirit, the Creator of the Universes, of the Etherean Worlds and are not of the corporeal worlds and the red planet—earth. For now, mankind comes in this part of its ego, proclaiming God-like power where they believe that they are masters over life and over death. They create in a dish a lamb, a pig, a horse, a child, and call it cloning or believe that they created life anew. For there, man believes that they need no God any longer and therefore God does not exist. And foolish and confused as these entities may be, as Looeamong who is the Buddha, the Mohammed, the Jesus, the Christs', for we, the messengers, the Angels, we warn you to not fall in this trap. For the one who has created the All, the perfect energy, is the Great God Jehovih, the magnificent God of Light. For millions of years, he was your Creator and will be for mil-lions of more years to come. I, your little messenger, forewarn you. Turn your back on all religious fads and return to the Creator or you will perish for all of eternity.

The
Etherean
Travellers
and the
Magical
Child

Chapter 14

As Life Forever Continues

I was walking and watching the shadow of my body fall upon the shoreline, along the lake. As I did hear the birds chirp and chatter, then I knew that one of my Etherean Friends was here. And then, my heart leaped from joy for, once again, I have my so-much-longed-for company here. Happily, we had a telepathic chatter. And I said, "Wow James! It's so wonderful to see you here. It has been a while. Could I ask you once more what shall happen during these times, since all of humanity seems to be entranced by the book of Revelations?" And he smiled. He said, "And has it made them change? Have they become more gentle, less war-like, respectful of all that lives and breathes, all that was created by the Great Spirit?"

And he said, "Do you really believe that there are so many writings among so many people on this Earth that it taught them that no

The
Etherean
Travellers
and the
Magical
Child

one owns anything? But you and I know, my little friend, that mankind must overcome their egos and learn to respect one another. So now, as they are all people of the Earth and we are speeding towards the Earth's renewal physically, the Earth shall look like a New World. But spiritually, the people will change their understanding too." Then, I asked, "How will they know that the time of the Creator has come?" "Then, my sweet," he said, "you be like the gentle breeze and cover the Earth from shore to shore, and you will tell them that now the time has come.

"It will be a time when no longer there shall be kings or queens, fierce men of government policing, or torturing conditions made by man to prevail upon this earth. For our Great Creator for so many centuries has foretold that this time was to unfold, where man must learn to police and control oneself. No more taxes to be collected from little people who starve. No more taxes to enforce upon people for wars and warfare to be had. No more needless killing for He has said thou shall not kill all that flies in the skies, creeps and crawls upon the fields, all that walks with their heads held up high. No manipulations or destroying and catching those who swim in the lakes, rivers and oceans. Food that will be eaten will be all clean and pure and shall not contain blood or spirit. For no man, medical or of government, will come to lord their will and power to say what one should eat, drink or partake in from that what was brought forth by the earth. *Everything that was grown by the Great Creator was put there for the benefit of beast and man.* And the Great Creator said that all of mankind was created equal, and in the new tomorrow, so it shall be; a place where no one shall be afraid of corrupt authority; no one in this time shall live in fear from one another; no dishonourable man or woman shall be able to take another's child, for all in the new tomorrow will live a peaceful and harmonious life. And all of mankind will be alike, living a life in spiritual balance, in honour of one another, and worshipping the Great Spirit, your Creator.

"So we will offer maps and safety guides for your survival, and wisdom for your new tomorrow. Learn to love one another. Tell them, my dearest child, that this is our message of respect and of honour. We wish all those from the red planet a good journey in spiritu-

The
Etherean
Travellers
and the
Magical
Child

ality and knowingness, and we advise you to stop all your wars. For, in the new tomorrow, you will sojourn with those who come from afar and other inhabited planets, for they are already amongst you, and with angels from on high.

"Now the time has arrived to go and find the Great Light. The Creator who said in these times when Looeamong has had his 3,000 years of reign, he then who is the Budha, and the Jesus is the very same and will go on the decline. And once more the earth's spiritual quest has come to an end when man has discovered that no one came to his beg and call and so they have learned their old beliefs have come to an end. And for those who still call out "Buddha, help me, save me," "Mohammed, where are you? Help me save me," and then man shall cry out, "Oh Jesus, oh Jesus, then you come and save me." And then they will know there is no other salvation than to return to the Great God, the Creator, who was there for all time. And then the quest will decline and vanish, and spirituality as you know it will no longer be, for man will wander hopelessly, feeling lost and without meaning. So then the time of the Great God of Light, the Jehovih of Old, will return into man's consciousness. So, first, then man will know all the false gods and deities before, once more, they can come to appreciate the Supreme Being of Old. And the universe knows that all angels will rejoice. They know now that humans will no longer be seeking to be followers of these who live in golden temples and who are supported by the rich of spirit and the materially poor. The seeker whose soul is thirsty for the truth will no longer need promises of a heaven offered by gurus, priests, rabbis and ministers only. Then, truly, my gentle spirit, they will know that through self-discipline and through being the best you can be, you can get to follow the Great Spirit, your Creator.

"For now the time has come, when man will come to know a polar shift. For the earth has started to rebel from the pollution of man's continuous destruction of the resources of this Red Planet. Now is the time man should come to realise the earth and the universe will suffer no more. All will come to readjust and return to splendour once more. A place where man must come to realise that how they think and how they act to one another, disregarding social status, race, creed,

The
Etherean
Travellers
and the
Magical
Child

or colour, that they all came from the same place. That all that flies in the sky, all that walks and creeps upon the land, and as well as all that is in the ocean has a memory bank and will remember all things great and small.

"For now, then, they can enjoy a new Earth and a new spirituality and thoroughly know what Peace means."

And then, he greeted me and told me a little chit-chat of where he has been. As he greeted me, I offered him this little poem:

From God's nature came the will of absolute burning Love
Then the Universe became truth and awakened to the splendour of
all creations unfolding Love
And perfect continuity and God in all awakened

And he then smiled and he gave his version of love:

Love is like a river, a stream that streams joyful on and on
The Soul is like a river, it glides on and on
My Soul is like a bird, it soars on wings so high
On to the Creator's Garden and there it sings on and on.

And so we greeted one another, and wished each other a sweet goodbye.

Once more I was alone. It was warm and sunny and the birds sang in the trees on high. The trees were dancing, whispering with their leaves, and I wished all a sweet goodbye.

116

A Soul

The
Etherean
Travellers
and the
Magical
Child

And the angels stood there,
And they smiled,
And so, one of the angels said, "So it be. Yeah, so it be,
So shall it be now and so on forever with everyone,
Yeah, everyone black as the night with a soul so white,
Red as the sunset, a soul truly on fire, shining like the sun on high,
White as snow, a heart of gold, platinum so we are told."
"Yeah, Yeah," they chanted. "Yes, all are one,
All our hearts are joined in one,
All our minds at rest and joined into one thinking, in unison, at
        peace with the all,
And so may all of you be in forever light."

—Thunderbird Woman

*The
Etherean
Travellers
and the
Magical
Child*

The Little Book That Could

Part 1: Messages From The Etherean Travellers

We, the Etherean Messengers, come to you to give you some of our wisdom and advice. We believe that, when the train is coming, one should step off the track. In places where your earth starts to shake, if you are desirous you can shake with it and see if you can survive. For you who have lived holy and spiritual lives, there is no fear, for life is forever. It is better than a meditation. Without an ending, it goes on and on until the day of blending with the Universal Light of Creation.

Shining on Your Journey

*So shining on your journeys through the all-ethereal space,
A radiator of warmth and light,*

Awakening beasts, birds, fish and mankind,
Seen and unseen,
All alike,
Oh God, like radiation, was there made by that what created.

The
Etherean
Travellers
and the
Magical
Child

James

Now I want to talk to you about giving away your power in the wrong directions by allowing others to suffocate and control your life. We advise every person in every country to go to your local parliament and receive your statutes of rights, especially in countries like the United States, Canada, and not to forget as well the people in Europe, and other continents of planet earth. If you do not exercise breathing and, all of a sudden, you breathe no longer, you keel over. If you are aware that you need to breathe to stay alive, then you come to a realisation that you must learn to exercise, as well as your breath, your rights, and understand your freedom.

Some of this information may come to some of you as a shock of awakening and create rebellion as well as despair. So if you do not care what is happening around you, and you give your power away to governments and religions, you are in the process of losing that what man and beasts treasure the most–freedom. Then the only thing you have is your thoughts and, let me tell you, my friend, that some governments in the world are developing these things that will infiltrate your very thoughts. Governments have been known throughout the ages to take out of the hands of all of its people that what they treasure most–freedom of action, freedom of thought and the freedom to decide what they should feed to their sick bodies, to either prolong or totally return it to full life.

I know what you are thinking: "How strange to find this kind of information in the back of a little book with spiritual content." But all of living and all of life is a spiritual action. So wonder no more, and let I, James, shake you wide awake.

Let us reach out to a part like Canada and open it up and see what the little people are perceiving when they have lost their freedoms and

The
Etherean
Travellers
and the
Magical
Child

their rights. Remember the medical profession, not too long ago, were a bunch of witches and herbalists, declared very dangerous to humanity. Start reading from the year 1400 and up and you will discover how many were burned at the stake as witches because the then society felt they had dangerous ideas. So for you who are in the medical profession, we, in the Angel world, call you to keep yourself in check and surrender your god-like attitude and the controlling over the bodies of all mankind.

You can't take away the freedoms of living, of the very essence of life, by forbidding or by taking away man's free will to use vitamins, vegetables, fruits, herbs, homeopathic medicines and acupuncture alike. So long as the Great Spirit creates new forests, valleys and fields to grow, so shall he create new supplements for man to have the knowledge to be well and survive. Do not take away from those who practise what you, at one time, practised. There are enough people out there who need to be well. For we, the Heavens, will watch you day and night.

Haida

My dearest friend, my name is Haida. I sojourned on the new Atlantean continent. I spent time visiting the Lemurians, the Martians, the Venusions, the Uranians, as well as the gods who reside on the planet Niburu. We have come to the conclusion, that returning here to earth, the earthly population has become into a control-freak type of thinking—in an uncanny, uncaring, uncompassionate, harsh, nerve-racking, "me" oriented and hateful lifestyle.

"Ho, ho," you say, "not all of us live like this." Well, my friend, you have given away your God-given freedom. You have given away your power to banks, and money institutions and governments alike. We warn you, you are speeding towards a time of evil world government, where everyone will be implanted with a computer chip with a day and date of a virus to be released into your bloodstream. When they feel you are no longer of any use, whether through illness or aging, your life they will undo. No free will will be left to you. Your world government was a thought that was created in 10 A.D. by King Herod and

120 Joseph Heli, the crown prince of the House of King David, with the sup-

port of the Roman Empire. It was later reinforced by Hitler, moved forward by Woodrow Wilson and is now coming into completion through the United Nations, under the guidance of the United States of America. The idea of world government is not to create world peace but rather to create a world-controlled economy and to suffocate the masses by taking away peoples' freedom of speech and movement.

In this place called Holy Land, by the name of Canada, you are suppressing all the ancient nations, their offsprings, and those who married thereupon, called the Metis Nation. The First Nations—many of them—are falling now into the material white man's trap. We urge all the red planet, as a nation, to unite and for all the Native Nations to also unite and to return to the old Algonquin way of understanding that all belongs to the Great Spirit and nothing belongs to man. Remember that when you call to go to the other plane, that what you call your body isn't even yours. So why fight war and be greedy? Do not allow governments of greed and war-like nature to raise up arms, nation against nation. Is it bloodthirst or is it just greed? Are these presidents and premiers, kings or queens, or Sultans as they may be, all in the arms-dealing or arms-manufacturing businesses? Or should they maybe get financial kickbacks or other material advantages, and so destroy man and nature to make your red planet unfit to exist?

I awake you to become active. Do not spy on one another. As you spy on one today, so be you the one who is spied on tomorrow. Do you realise that Crime Stoppers came from the German SS time of Hitler. Do not report and take down, in a moment of anger, your neighbour. For when tomorrow comes and life is gone as you know it, you will come face to face with your accused or your accuser in the other realm. In a country as rich as this nation, and nations all over the globe in similar situations, you must remember who are supporting them. We pray that you all discard your credit cards, claim your power back, as given to you by the Great Creator, the Great Spirit of Four Directions in the Universe. You have come in a time when you cannot trust or believe, from those who police you, to those who proclaim they are in control.

Wake up, my dearly beloved, for the time of total global renew-

*The
Etherean
Travellers
and the
Magical
Child*

al is at hand. Reach out to the so-called disenfranchised—the poor, wherever they may be. Truly practise love one another, as far and near as they may be. Do make sure that you clear from your heart all pain, hatred and anger. Forgive the ones who raised you, for even they will have suffered great pain. Stop inflicting your garbage throwing, your rudeness and unkindness to man, beast, earth and universe. Learn to do your own self-policing. Remember, in the courts of man, justice is only in the mind of the beholder.

I wish you to look upon the sky and welcome those from Saturn, Niburu (the planet of the gods), Venus, Mars and Jupiter, who are now sojourning your earthly space. Open your hearts, reach out in prayer. Heavenly ships have landed nearby in the sky. Many descensions to the earth are taking place and many ascensions are going on and on. No, people do not just go missing. Some have desired to not return to earth. When I come with a different writing, I will tell you of that from the First Resurrection, the Second Resurrection, the Third Resurrection. And I must tell you, before I go, when many sojourn in their space ships, and you in your rocket-powered cigars, no, no, you cannot reach us. We see you. We are beyond the stars. You do not have the power to see all dimensions and that will maintain our peace, joy and love. For all of light, He is the Great Creator. And He will keep creating on and on. Greetings from Commander Haida who came to you from beyond the stars.

The Creator

*The Creator's laws of truth and heaven now were born the laws of
        right and wrong consciousness,
In actions, choices to be made by holy man,
Then conscious fervour set all on fire,
The forests in late sunlight all ablaze,
A lake with gentle breezes waving in the stillness of good night,
In angels' arms now resting till morning came God's ever bright.*

122

Kiryon

Hello. Now is my turn to speak to you. And I speak to you out of great compassion. Keep your beauty and, above all, good health. Eat daily all you need dears, from fruit, vegetables, vitamins and root plants and air, on and on. And take all the vitamins you need, the herbals that were put there to make you strong. And teach your medicals to love and respect you, as you will honour them for who they are. It was a glorious time to help to get some of our words out and it filled my wonderful heart with joy. And when you sit sometime alone in meditation, just call me on and on. And when you smell gardenias, and see blue lights flying through your room, I say hello. And then, I am gone. Goodbye.

Love Are Beams

Oh love are beams who are sent towards the Creator, the beholder
      of all who lives,
He who holds all knowledge,
Of all alive he gave sun to behold,
The all in golden rays.

Ahtmar

A small greeting from a great friend. Hang in there, you all. Keep meditating. Do breathing exercises and keep your spirit great and tall. Good wishes, much health from me. Just call Ahtmar....com

Sophia

Hey, hey. I am Sophia and I just come to say hello and float through and say I'll send many good thoughts and create with my thoughts wonderful things. Remember, we taught you thoughts are things. Keep up the positive. Hold onto your control. Nurture your power. And me too, call me ...com

The
Etherean
Travellers
and the
Magical
Child

Alika

Hi. Ho Hi. That's me. Wishing you a happy realisation, a journey that will set you free, and then free at last to protest against warring and hatred, even though they like to bind you. The earth in motion, set by the Great God of Light, will set you free. Send good thoughts, good energies. Be the best you can be. And hey, hey, if you need me, say Hi Ho, Alika ...com

Mr. James

I, James, say hello to all of you earthbound and to you who soon will be free. Planet earth or, we should say, the red planet, becomes quickly now spaceship earth. Hang tight, don't engage in that what isn't morally right. Need not to lie out of fear, to shout or beat each other, or hate the other one. Understanding and wisdom, swiftness of mind are needed to go into survival mode. Be clear. Do not say that what you do not mean. Respect one another. I appreciated all of your time. I thank you for reading all our writings. Hope that you did understand our teaching from afar. Remember again, all action has consequences, cause and effect. May your actions be compassionate and peaceful. May you rebel against all that is wrong and have honour and live with respect, knowing there is no violence needed. Just start to correct all the wrongs.

I advise you to change your justice system so they learn to judge really what is wrong. Advise them to re-enter through humanity into a system that has all gone wrong. No judges and lawyers making deals with one another and assessing to let go the one who has material status, and then declaring the little innocent one wrong for the sake of the rich, guilty one. Re-check your policing systems and check them carefully out. Who did train them and where did they come from? Did they bring techniques and intimidations from your World War II, long gone? "Now, now," you say, "we did not know that you heavenly beings would be so aware." Yes, we have a memory as long as time, and forever forward. We know the schemings that went and will come. To hire the ex-Nazi perpetrators to set up your policing systems, is your memory that far gone that you can't remember the sufferings and atrocities that went on over Europe?

I will speak to you to refreshen all of your memories and give knowledge to your young to know that the World War II techniques are still going on and on. Their intimidations, their surveying, their spying, so-called information-gathering about everyone, is still going on. Invasions of privacy are continually going on. It is more sophisticated than you thought? You ask, "What nonsense I am speaking?" Let me point out to you what really is going on. Electromagnetic-powered discs on radar frequencies are floating over your homes. Helicopters with infrared photography are surveying each and every building, boats and cars, scanning over fields and meadows to control to the so-called 'goings on.' Soon, they will install parking metres in each and every city and town to allow you to use credit or debit cards. They will do this to supposedly relieve you of the bother of carrying money, but will actually be controlling to know your comings and goings.

Technology makes it possible, without you knowing, to tap into your phone conversations, to clear out your hard drive disks from your computer, to check to whom you communicate. Technology invented for archeological digs are used to dig on you, to see what is in your homes, apartments, or where you are living, and conducting your businesses too. They will scan and check your mail, my friend. Ho, ho, your thrown-away garbage too. If your hydro or water bill is higher than before, be sure you will be reported and they will show up at your door. You call that crime-stopper? This is your freedom you've lost from before. How do you feel when you live on the 20th floor, my dear, and a disc, not to be so easily detected by you, flew by your windows and photographed everything inside? Are you surprised a little yet? Are you aware that the global crime rate is only 2%? This kind of surveillance is not for your protection.

The Royal Canadian Mounted Police was reconstructed right after the end of the Second World War. They constructed a new system set up by the NSB, the civilian security police. Their knowledge

*The
Ethrean
Travellers
and the
Magical
Child*

and training also were introduced into the CIA and the FBI in the United States—ruthless spying and invading the space of whomever they like to spy on, to harass and intimidate. Worldwide, we, from the other worlds, know so. On many occasions in Canada, USA and Haiti, were techniques used, taught by the former NSB, the Hitler regime. Far-fetched you will say, the war is long over. Yeah, yeah I hear you, but listen to this, my friend.

Oh wait, I have more for you. At one time, in a downtown Canadian city, I went for a stroll around the 11th hour. A man, a woman and a child in a carriage be. As there suddenly the Gestapo, oh pardon me, walked up to this young couple going home after work. They were stopped, verbally harassed and physically the young man against the wall was ploughed. The young woman, in fear, started calling and he felt protect I must my child, my wife, my own being. A skirmish happened and a social worker arrived immediately upon the scene. A passer-by stood still, young and strong, and observed the scene. One of the Gestapos asked him, was he a lawyer who was on the scene, upon which the young man said, "What you are doing is against the Canadian Constitution and human rights. You are trampling all over the constitution, which gives Canadians freedoms and rights," upon which swiftly the Gestapos retreated. And I watched all of them go into the night. As if you were thinking you were living in a lovely and harmonious land, and nothing alike the former Soviet Union communistic regime where the government at any time could enter your place, grab and arrest you, the same as with the Gestapo in World War II. Be aware that your freedoms in Canada and the United States of America are totally eroded.

Here my friend, right in Canada, there were owners of health food stores who found themselves, during nighttime hours, parts of raids—Gestapo-way attacks. They were thrown against the walls and beaten up, and held at gunpoint. Their houses were ransacked and torn apart, searching for supplies of vitamins and herbals actually not illegal by law. A moral insult to the nation of freedom, so the people thought. Awaken, awaken, do not allow this to go on. Your freedoms are taken and soon it will all be gone. "Oh," you say, "what is that of my business? Vitamins I use not. Herbals I have no need of. I could never be in such a spot." Do you have a business or do you work a lot? There is another form of Gestapo—the ones called 'tax-a-lots.' They came to one who drafted buildings, houses and bridges a lot. Even government buildings were on his easel a lot. He needed to collect his monies from whom he had worked a lot. And governments are slow in paying. Never mind, there came the tax-a-lots, and they went in to his children's accounts—the students who were still in school. The wife and her mother were robbed in their bank accounts by the tax-a-lots. The upset caused him to die. The stress became too great to watch his family suffer and their lives went to pot. And that is not meaning hemp! I tell you, taxes are very evil. Throughout of history, it has crushed economies and lands and man. But in this land, its constitution did not give a right to the tax-a-lots to collect from innocent citizens since, in the Constitutions of Canada and the United States of America, it does not appear. So ask for your freedoms and don't let the tax-a-lots near. King Herod is long dead and his laws are outdated. No taxes creates work and solid economies.

I will speak about what has been done to the First Nations—its people. First, they were abused and used by the religious ones and were called savages no matter how wise and in great spiritual balance they were. They became trampled on and cheated and lied to by the government of the day. Then there came the Gestapo with their prejudices, hatreds, narrow-minded, uneducated behaviour who trampled upon those, the custodians of this very land, who never polluted, destroyed, or corrupted mother earth. In time, everything for the first people who came to this earth, this part of the world, became a time of hardship and confusion because of white man's law—a law so adjustable to likes and dislikes, it victimized and drove women, children and man into the ground, making them think they were worthless—the children of the Great Spirit of Old.

Let me tell you this story, this story we watched from on high. Actually it is two stories. The first one is of the 56-year-old native man from a proud tribe, a son of a shaman's father. This son was picked up by the Gestapo. He was very cold and his legs were stiff from sit-

*The
Etherean
Travellers
and the
Magical
Child*

ting and waiting for the bus. It was winter in Alberta. He was yanked off the sidewalk as if he was terribly drunk, and thrown in their paddy wagon. Punched, kicked and beaten, he lost most of the teeth out of his mouth. His ribs were crushed and broken. And then he was driven in the paddy wagon out of town to be tossed out of the paddy wagon onto a lonely country road. Lucky we angels came looking and alerted the farmer and his dog at a nearby house. And, so, his life became saved now and he lived out his life on the reserve.

What do you feel, my dearest ones, if it was your mother who was so hungry and cold, became arrested and was in her pregnancy nine months gone? It was so-called 'a mistake,' but she had been arrested and had struggled against them. She was punched, kicked and beaten and so gave birth to a child who was dead. What must we angels tell you what man can do to man? We teach you, do not judge them, but do whatever you can to change it. We are not in place to be your accusers. When you leave a young person 16 years of age, lying with barely a blanket in a doorway upon the street, hungry and cold, ask yourself, what had she done. In great pain and misery, she lay there as you, the humans, walk on and on. Your so-called 'social assistance,' from the British Columbia New Democratic Party, elected by the people-a-lot, not caring, not daring to pay to the starving and the hungry-a-lot. And you ask, "Can you prove it?" Well, I can prove that vouchers, meal tickets, from your Department of Human Resources, with the name of Finance Division, located at P.O. Box 5051, Station Main, Vancouver, BC, V6B 4A9, are given to the disenfranchised, or let us call them the poor ones—whether they are the 16, 14, 21, or 30-year old ones, or, for that matter, the 64-year-old ones too, the victims of a mismanaged economy called good-for-everyone. These vouchers came to a value of $6.50, to live on over a four-day period. There was no concern whether there was shelter or even a blanket. The young person ended up on the streets.

And so I ask you if you think it can be done, to take yourself and your teenagers, be out of your home or shelter, and take a blanket to a doorway upon the street. Be hungry and cold, and ask yourself, "What have we done to live in great pain and misery to lay in a

The
Etherean
Travellers
and the
Magical
Child

doorway hungry and cold?" as you, the other humans, walk on and on. Upon the street, hungry and cold, they feel totally abandoned and what had the poor ones, the disenfranchised ones, done? In great pain and misery they lay there as you NDP'ers, Reformers, Liberals and Conservatives walk on and on. There are so many who are broken and live in total pain and are forced to live in underground parking and parks on and on. Do you give them no shelter, no love, no hope, no food so they can live in their tomorrow? Neither clothing for them to go on and on? Remember, some day there could be this stranger, an angel, knocking on your heart on and on, to awaken if you have left a consciousness for humanity. So you, one day, peacefully can live on and on. A country so rich in resources sold out to banking and corporations, controlling the governments and the governments are trampled upon. As puppets, they are responding to demands by the credit card mongers to take away freedom of trading in a world controlled by a gun. Your land, where the rich will become richer and the rest are all the poor ones. In warm countries, survival is still a possibility, but in the cold and wetlands, no survival for everyone goes on and on.

There are so many who are broken, live in pain and must so live on. Do you give them no shelter, no love, no hope, no food, neither clothing for them to go on? Remember, some day you could be this little stranger needing work or a rod to fish.

So we from the Etherean Worlds ask you to reclaim your power. We have come to bring you awareness, to gain a powerful life and

The
Etherean
Travellers
and the
Magical
Child

truly peace profound for where one cannot be harassed, threatened or hassled, that place truly attained peace profound.

And we will bring you another lovely incident of the fortunes that you have lost from your freedoms and your peace of mind. As an Asian-Canadian was driving after closing his business at 4:30pm that night, the Gestapos were bored and had been lingering on a mountain road that very night. They didn't like the way he looked and called him over closer in sight. The man from Asian descent, confused, not understanding, was beat up by them that very night. Innocent, not knowing his constitution, he left in fear into the night.

A scanner is appointed for use to hear your conversations, so be careful to not speak on your phone about anything that later can be used by your government to harass you, to hurt you, to put you down, to take away your peaceful goodnight. If you not immediately obey to their commands, whether they are wrong and you are right, a gun will be drawn and pointed, and maybe beat up you will be. No searches from Gestapos are legal. Read your constitution or whatever you call it. Know your rights wherever you may be. Create an atmosphere of protection—good and wise family and friends. There is strength in numbers. A free land allows you to protest, to voice your thoughts and opinion in peaceful manner. I warn you, do not lose that right. We, heavenly beings, believe that you have lost your freedoms and we call you out of your slumber and seek your spiritual and God-given right. For He—the Great Spirit—said, "For all nations, for all beings have that right of peace and harmony and to live an undisturbed, hunger-free and peaceful life. Let no man from the universe or upon earth take away my given freedoms."

I, James, I wish you to learn and understand no greater freedom than to choose your spiritual journey, to live upon earth with all races and creatures under the banner of the Great God Jehovih, without war, suppression. And killing for food, bird, fish and beast is forbidden, for a world without murder is a world filled with peace.

James speaking for the Great God of Light. And I, Mr James can be reached under .com.com.com and it will arrive. Peace unto all.

James.

We Are All Judges

We are all gods who judge,
The self when the time has come,
To go before the all are God,
So let us live according to God's will,
And we are all truly judges,
And become as one.

*The
Etherean
Travellers
and the
Magical
Child*

Truth

A Wake-up Call for Religion

The sun is rising upon the year 2000, according to Christianity's count of time. The new millennium will bring the return of the Creator. A light is shining upon Christianity and other religions, and the Creator and the angel world are unearthing truths globally.

The time has come for people to come to the realisation that religion, as it was designed during the time of King Herod the First, has undergone a major change. No longer is it seen the way it was in ancient Judaic times of that day. A new form of Judaism, known today as Christianity, was born in 10AD.

The Royal Family, from the House of King David, ruled Judea at the time. Joseph Heli was the crown prince who was next in the royal bloodline to become the new King David. But King Herod the First was sent from Rome to rule over the entire area and the House of David. In those days, the high priests and popes had long hair, ringlets and beards while those out of the royal families wore short hair and had no beards. This appearance set the royalty apart. King Herod was the original inventor of taxes, and as a convert to a new Judaic religion (Christianity), he arranged with apostles to conduct the first census in the area in for the purposes of tax collection. People living today are the victims of the high tax system that was created by the Herods in that century.

The House of David hoped that King Herod would allow them a section of land in Judea to rule. This never happened. During this time, Joseph and his wife Mary were expecting another child, who would join his siblings, Joseph of Arimathea and Mary. They planned for this child to be born in September, as this would qualify the child to be the new crown prince of the House of David. Jesus and his twin brother James (later known as Isukiri) were born in the house of the Queen's (Mary's) mother in Qumran. The birth took place during the reign of the high priest, Simon Boethus. The birth of James was kept secret. He was smuggled out and taken to Japan. In those days having twins was considered evil. King Herod found out about the birth and sent out a party of men to find the Royal Family. When Joseph and Mary heard about this, they left with their children and moved into Egypt.

Humanity has been told for the past 2000 years that Jesus was born in a stable and that he was a poor carpenter's son. In reality, Jesus' father was official crown prince of the throne of King David and Jesus was born in a palace. Jesus' brother James, who was first born of the twins, was the real successor to the throne but was passed over in favour of Jesus. Jesus received most of his training and education as a Judaic royal prince by the high priests in the Judaic temple, while Isukiri was trained as a royal prince in Japan. Jesus was further educated through his travels with Joseph in Japan, India, China, Turkey and Egypt. As part of his education, Jesus was programmed to become a religious leader and social rebel. When he went to Japan, he landed in an area that is now known as Noto Peninsula in the Ishikawa Prefecture. He walked 50 kilometres from there to his imperial ancestors' Grand Shrine, which has now been moved to Isohara. He spent 8 years in Japan studying Shinto disciplines to develop his mystical understanding and power.

Joseph and the high priests from the Judaic temple devised a plan for Joseph to regain control over his country as King of the House of David, as well as control over the world. This was to be done by revising the Judaic religion to accept Gentiles, converting people to the new religion and making it accessible to all, thereby gaining world control.

They ran into opposition to this from a young man by the name of John the Baptist. John was a holy person who taught people and baptised them under the ancient laws of Moses and Zarathustra. He disapproved of what they had done with the ancient laws of Judaism and the laws of the Creator—Jehovih.

Two Popes were in power in Judea at the time. They were part of the plan to use the new religion to gain political power. Menasseh thought he could overthrow the Herods through war. Jesus was used to a great extent by the Samaritans to gather people to back up and support Manasseh's wish. However, Jesus did not want to align himself with war. Menahem, who was the original instigator of the change

*The
Etherean
Travellers
and the
Magical
Child*

and the break-up of the split up of ancient Judaism, was looking to create a following and eventually gain back the control over the area of that day. Jesus used his social and religious empowerment to create followers so that he could back up the desire of Menahem to create a new Judea, and thus world control.

Jesus was never seen as having special holy power while he was growing up or when he had followers, but was respected as a royal for his kindness. During the time that Jesus was gathering followers (and thereby votes), his brother Isukiri returned to the area and helped with the teachings and gathering of support in areas where Jesus had not been. This explains why it was said that Jesus appeared in more than one place at a time.

To give you a tidbit, also during this time (AD 32), at age 36, Jesus married 27 year-old Mary Magdalene. She was pregnant when they married and gave birth to a girl child in September, AD 33. (Read the marriage story in the Bible). And anyone who is interested in John the Baptist and his involvement with Mary Magdalene and Jesus' mother, both of whom were followers of his teachings of Eastern Judaic and Zarathustrian laws, please read the Qumran Scrolls, and the writings of Mark, the apostle, and you will see the involvement of Jesus in the death of John the Baptist.

Meanwhile, the political movement Jesus was involved with went awry and the popes and high priests wanted to get Jesus out of the way, as he no longer served their purposes. Jesus left the Middle East for Egypt, while his brother ended up being arrested in his place. Isukiri was the one who was crucified and taken to a tomb originally set aside for his brother, Joseph of Arimathea. He was treated there but later died from complications of the crucifixion. He was embalmed and laid to rest in the tomb. Meanwhile, Jesus had secretly returned to see his twin brother. On one occasion Jesus was seen by his followers exiting the tomb, thus creating the story of his resurrection.

Jesus arranged with Joseph of Arimathea to take Mary Magdalene and his children to France, while Jesus tied up his affairs. Since he was 'resurrected', he became an untouchable. He went to France to join his wife and children but quickly abandoned them to travel the world, eventually ending up in Japan in Herai Village, which is in the Northern part of the country. He returned to Judea to take Isukiri's remains back to Japan for burial. In Japan, he rejoined some of his followers who were later instrumental in starting the Prior du Sion, which in the year 1300 became known as the Masons. Jesus lived in Japan and married again, having 3 additional children. His son died as a young child. His daughters married and lived in Japan, and populated a village that, even today, still lives by and celebrates Judaic law. His male descendants looked like him. Jesus died at the age of 106 and was buried in Herai beside his brother. The evidence, which supports Jesus' burial, can be found in the Takenouchi Documents in Japan. Moslems are aware of the true story of Jesus and his time in Japan, hence the hatred of the Christian controllers towards the Moslem faith.

When Jesus left Judea for Japan, Simon Magus came into power as a new pope of Judaic Christianity and he continued what Joseph Heli had started in terms of world government, which was the birth of the New World Order we hear of today. It is Judaic Christianity, the Masons and a small fraction of others, who are part of an elite group that currently controls the world and its economies.

The chrysanthemum is the emblem of the Imperial House of Japan and it holds within it the emblem of the House of King David (mogendavid). Christianity adopted the chrysanthemum used by Jesus and his family, and it appears above their temples and church doors.

As you can see, whether you do so with or without rebellion, Jesus was a human being who was seriously used for political and religious purposes. Be aware that hundreds and hundreds of millions of people all over the earth have died terrible deaths under the rule and reign of what was created during those days. Because of the terrible lies, suppression and abuse shown by religions throughout the ages, even today we see people die for religion's sake and for the power of those that are in control. We respect the life of the man Jesus, but to us he was no God. And sorry we must be for all those who were needlessly killed when others were made to believe there was something to defend–called religion. Also, when you pay your taxes, think about King Herod and his alliance with new Judaism which is now called Christianity.

If only mankind can come to grasp that it is high time to stop all this hatred and to return to the Creator of Old. It is time to realise that you do not need to fatten the weapon dealers' bank accounts, nor those of governments who deal in weaponry. Go and read the works of Zarathustra and Confucius, and study the ancient scripts that are left of the original Judaism. Overstep the barriers of racism and come truly to respect the earth and all that lives upon it, within it, and above it. It is time to also realise that you do not need to fatten-up the church coffers when globally they offer so little of their total financial resources for people in need. Expensive, tax-free church basements stand empty while the Creator's children are left hungry and cold, fending for themselves on the streets. Religious organisations proclaim to be charitable but charge street people to stay in their facilities. Where do they expect these people to raise the money for shelter? What man does to man in the name of religion makes the Creator and Angel world weep.

You must also wake-up to the food you eat, where it comes from, and if there was any suffering involved in obtaining it. Christianity and Buddhism have never come to understand that the Creator gave the law that said, "Thou shalt not kill that which walks, creeps, crawls upon the earth, flies in the sky and swims in the rivers and oceans. For all that lives, I gave my devine breath of air. Thou shalt not kill." Man should become aware of the words "Thou shalt not kill." Even those who have chosen Buddhism as their religion cannot excuse themselves by the certain way the moon is in the sky—that it is then okay to kill and eat meat. People who are meat eaters eat of fear, pain and suffering, and of death and dying. How can they be not war-like when their DNA is programmed with death, dying and suffering? People who are proclaimed by the masses to be holy also indulge in the eating of fowl, fish and meat. The current Pope and Dalai Lama are not vegetarians.

We are also informing you about the enormous rise of Buddhism and Moslem faiths in our current times. However, Christians, Buddhists and Moslems are soon going to be joining hands and will become one family under one god, Yahweh. We have seen for the last 1800 years this eventual coming together of major religions under the power of this lower god, Yahweh.

We have also seen the enormous tragedy of humanity having turned away from the Creator—the energy who creates and recreates and continually supplies sustenance, life and goodness with its breath of life. This is the Great God of Love and Light who creates no war and hatred—a Creator who watches the ever-expanding world control and sees the fearful masses of poor, starving and sick children and adults. In places where religion is so rich and powerful, the religions still ask for money from even the little people who have almost nothing. Even Jesus himself would reel at what the religion that he helped create has become. It is religion that thrives on creating fear, and gains its financial empowerment through fear and manipulation of the masses. It must pain Jesus to know that his name has been used for 2000 years to create guilt, fear and death. It must stop.

There are many people who live in fear of passing to the next world and believe that they have to pay off a god and angel world to get a place in heaven. If your god is so corrupt that you can buy a place or a good existence according to the donation you make on your last moment of life, what kind of god is he? And what kind of god is a god of hate that allows its followers and institutions to put so many in such fear of an ending world, which the religious fear-mongers of today promote in seeking financial gains?

My advice to all the peoples of the earth is to return to your Creator. Mend your ways by becoming compassionate, thoughtful, tolerant and helpful to one another. Banish untruths and greed. For then truly you have nothing to fear in the new millennium. Do not just talk about loving one another—learn to live the love and be within your spirit. It is not the practice of religion, but rather the practice of true spirituality that raises one's soul up to the Creator.

My communications in the future will be at lectures conducted by Thunderbird Woman.

Greetings from Truth.

*The
Etherean
Travellers
and the
Magical
Child*

Part 2: Earth Changes

We are going to make you aware that you are living in a time of great renewal, of global awakening.

And there is a great possibility of you experiencing, like those of old, a total polar shift, a movement of Northeast going Southwest. Therefore, south shall become north and north becomes south and the deserts will bloom again. If you are well aware, you will have noticed the great climatic changes, that your winter no longer starts at the same time, as neither does spring. And some of you feel that you have lost summer. The earth, because of the great abuse it has endured, can no longer endure the suffering it is experiencing. If you take an apple and pull a string through the apple and you start to bore away parts of the apple, you will see that the apple will start to tip. If you take all the fluids out, the apple will start to dry up in certain areas and, in other areas it will decay. If we drained the blood out of a human being and we robbed him of his air, very soon he will die off. If we keep taking and polluting at the same rate as it happens today, because of greed, egotistical living, then soon the must-haves will discover they have none. You can only strip so many trees, rip out so much oil and coal, minerals and precious stones. How much gold, how many jewels does one need?

If you allow someone to make it impossible for you to breathe and to take everything that keeps you afloat, like natural gases, then you crash. You can make a good try by filling a balloon and it will become nice and round and it will float. As we have just recently seen, great men with their helium tanks and balloons, attempting to float across the earth but crashing in the end because of a leak in the helium line. Please do not believe that you are in El Niño because you would have been in El Niño for the last 4 years, had it been true, since March 24, 1994. This is when the mother energy and the Aquarian energy came into their being. The outer crust of the earth has gone into its slippage and movement because the earth itself is contracting under it due to the stripping of its resources. El Niño started in 1997, but your major disasters of flooding, rain, snow and ice storms started in the fall of 1994, giving you evidence of the on-going polar shift and the earth crust movement.

We are going to go to the area of Canada, Alaska and the North Atlantic Ocean down to the North Pacific Ocean. If you take a map and lay the map down and have a coloured pencil or pen, you can circle or make stars in the areas that we give you. Starting off in the area of Nome, Alaska—a very volatile landmass—earthquake activity throughout Alaska will be quite high, especially from Nome to Fairbanks to Anchorage. Part of the higher tip of the Yukon, as well. There will be major volcanic activity in your area as we are giving you this timeline from 1997 onward throughout the year 2008—a time span of ten years. So for you who live close to the volcano, be wise and try to move or situate yourself into a safety area if you so desire, since your area of Alaska is due for serious industrial accidents of chemical or nuclear origin. Our saying is, "when the train is coming, get off the track."

Then we move on to the lower part of the Yukon, towards BC and Alberta. The area is quite safe. The Northwest Territories will become a favourable place to live, past the year 2006.

139

Now we are going down to BC. The lower part of Vancouver Island is an extremely dangerous place to be for earthquakes and tidal waves alike. And so remember, also, that the smaller islands are in danger of earth movement and tsunamis as well. We go to the mainland of BC. The higher part of BC, especially higher up on the Alberta side, is quite stable—some minor earth tremors, but plagues of pests will endanger the food supply, due to the sudden warming up of the land. Vancouver itself and the Lower Mainland will experience a great deal of flooding, serious earth tremors and earthquakes, and will run a great risk of being overrun by a tsunami, especially from the 14th of February, 1998 to September, 2001. The higher risk for the coastlines of Vancouver Island, and the western coast of British Columbia mainland from Prince Rupert down to White Rock, is of erosion and continual earth movement, shaking loose the fragile coastline, causing it to drop into the ocean. Your earthquake risk is increasing and, for those who live in Richmond, BC, it would be wise to leave the area. Crying over spilled milk has no use.

We go on to the province of Alberta. The province will experience major droughts and the area of Calgary and Lethbridge, to Medicine Hat, will experience serious earthquake activities and, in later time, during the time of the polar shift, they will see waters rise and ocean shores form. By the year 2020, they will have seen this come about. Northern Alberta will be a safe area.

Moving on to Saskatchewan, it will experience major pestilence and droughts. Northern Saskatchewan, like northern Alberta, will also be a safe area. Later, during the polar shift, water will come into Saskatchewan and, once more, the saying, "Tie your boat up in Saskatchewan," will become a reality. However, Saskatchewan will, in the end, become the food basket of the world.

Morden, Manitoba to Winnipeg and its surrounding area, will be extremely dangerous. Flooding, earth movement, cyclones and tornadoes will be in evidence. Also, there is a risk of nuclear fallout.

In Ontario, plagues of pestilence, major floods, and disastrous weather conditions will prevail in 1998, 1999 and up to the year 2008. Snowstorms in uncanny amounts will occur out of season. The

Ottawa, Toronto and Montreal areas are all extremely dangerous places to be—inundated with water and earth movement. Major disasters of weather, tornadoes, lightening storms due to climatic changes, will occur throughout the province. The area from Northern Ontario through to Manitoba is a safety area. Also, in Ontario, there will a danger of fallout from existing nuclear reactors by 2008.

In Quebec, Montreal will also be inundated with water and experience major earth movement. There are a number of safety areas in Northern Quebec. 1998 through 2001 will be very difficult years throughout Quebec weatherwise, including great heat waves, and lightening and thunder storms.

These are parts of Canada saying to you that all of you internationally will have to become prepared. If you decide you want more information about earth changes world-wide, please contact:

e-mail: ahtmar1@CosmicEnergyExperience.com

Be Like a Star

Be like a star,
And shine below God's throne,
To be seen by all of mankind,
To remember that God is home.

*The
Etherean
Travellers
and the
Magical
Child*

Part 3: Disaster Preparedness

We, the Etherean Travellers and myself, are going to provide you with a workable, and hopefully, understandable guide to supplies required to fill your first needs for survival in the event of a disaster.

Tips on What to Do Before a Disaster Happens

If you live alone, we would like you to prepare an emergency plan for yourself. It is also advisable for families to prepare a plan, including how to stay in contact..

We advise you to seek a first aid course in your neighbourhood, city or town. Learn cardiopulmonary resuscitation (CPR).

Prepare a backpack. Make a list of emergency phone numbers and other document numbers you may need to reference, and place it in the backpack. For the people who live in warm countries, and for you who do not, a number one thing is to have soap and toothpaste stored in your pack. If you wear glasses or contact lenses, place an extra set in it as well. It is advisable for each and everyone who prepares a backpack, whether for hiking, camping or travel, but especially for disaster preparedness, to have a bottle of Rescue Remedy available in it. This can be purchased in natural and holistic supply stores. Rescue Remedy is a natural substance and, when a person is in shock, a couple of drops will take a person out of that state of shock. The stores can also supply you with an emergency first aid homeopathic kit. Don't forget that if you are on various medications you pack them as well. Include some water, food, clothing and selective emergency supplies as discussed below.

Find where the safe places are to be and where not to be. Make a small map. Colour the danger areas red and the safe areas green. Hang it next to your backpack at the door as a reminder so you do not get trapped in the wrong places.

When people are in earthquakes or tsunamis, they sometimes become disoriented. Therefore, practise going to your safe place many times. Do this at least four times a month, two times during night-time and two times during daytime. Safe places are under very heavy tables, well-constructed desks, inside hallways, corners of rooms, or under strong archways. Very dangerous places are near windows, mirrors and under heavy objects that can fall from kitchen cupboards, bookcases or other shelving. Other dangerous areas include the centre of a room, the area near a gas outlet or next to the chimney. Be careful where the stove, and the refrigerator with its contents, can slide or tumble across the floor. Please pay attention to your doorways since, during the shaking, the doors can slam on you and hurt you. If you have a family living with you, prepare them as well, and practise often especially where there are small children or elderly involved. Hang a list on your refrigerator door so you have a plan accessible to everyone. Write down if there are those of you who need to take medications, such as insulin or heart medications. Keep the medications within easy reach. Don't forget to include on your list to help people who are homebound, as well as animals.

Go around the apartment building you live in, or your home, and check for weak points on the ground and the structure itself. Make note of these. If your house is built on a mountainside, make sure it is

*The
Etherean
Travellers
and the
Magical
Child*

bolted to the foundation and to the mountainside itself. Make sure the weaker walls are braced. Check your chimney to ensure that it is strong and well braced. Take some plywood and put it around your chimney in the attic so that the debris and chunks of concrete do not come crashing through your ceiling and kill or injure you. Take the time to tie down your hot water heater, and bolt your washer, dryer, stove and fridge to the floor or the wall. Otherwise, for example, a gas stove may leak gas into your home and cause an explosion.

Have a wrench and pliers available near your furnace or gas-line. Also, stabilise your furniture, bookcases, glass cabinets, etc., so they cannot fly off the wall and tumble on top of you. Put the heavier books on the bottom shelves so they will not tip. Affix mirrors, paintings, and other hanging objects to the wall. In your kitchen, keep heavy, breakable items on the bottom shelves of cabinets. Purchase childproof locks to keep the kitchen cupboards secure. Locate your bed and chairs away from chimneys and windows. Make sure that you do not place a baby's crib next to a window, as you never know when an earthquake will occur. Please don't hang pictures or mirrors above your bed. If you have curtains or drapery in front of your windows, the window panes or window glass will not immediately fall upon your head if you are sitting next to the window. They will also stop broken glass from falling and scattering all over the floor. Keep flammable items and household items such as paint cans, pressurised spray cans or hairspray, away from heat sources where there is a possibility of combustion, since items could spill and create a large fire.

Arrange for earthquake insurance and really check out that the insurance company can guarantee your losses during the time of flood, tsunami, and earthquake. Assemble a home emergency supply kit. List all the needs of your family members on the inside of your kit. Make the kit large enough so it can supply possible others, as well. Store your emergency supplies, such as dry baby clothes, sweaters, T-shirts, socks and whatever you need or may need, in a plastic bag, under a stairway or close to your exit door. Have a fire extinguisher located there as well. It might not be possible for you to drive your automobile, bicycle or motorbike, but equip them with an emergency kit too. If you have a tool shed, equip it with necessary emergency supplies. We are advising that when you are in a state of shock, you need to have already prepared what you will first require in the disaster situation. Also, as experienced by others who have lived through disasters, it is necessary that you have the essential emergency supplies you need (eg medication, drinking water, Rescue Remedy) stored in two different places. For you who are living in low-lying areas, either sew or purchase your own sandbags. It doesn't hurt to have a supply of sandbags on hand. You can make them out of old bed sheets, slings and bandages.

We want you to go to your local supermarket and purchase large drinking water containers, filled with purified water. Although there is a belief that a person needs four litres of water per day, that is not quite so with those who have been in earthquakes. The tendency seems to be that six to seven litres is more like it. Keep the water in a dark place. Recycle it. In your backpack, have a bottle or two of drinking water available for each family member. Label each bottle as to when it was first filled. For you who are deciding to bottle drinking water from the tap, be careful. For storage of uncontaminated tap water, put four drops of bleach in a large container or three drops in a medium sized container. You may have to put bleach in your drinking water to decontaminate it. Put in three drops of the chlorine bleach per litre of contaminated water. Shake it, stir it and let it stand for three to four hours. It would be good to use non-perfumed chlorine bleach that you can purchase at your local drugstore. You can also buy water purification tablets there. All water can also be made safe by boiling it for ten minutes. If you need water, you can also count on using the water from your hot water boiler. Make sure that you have enough drinking water for your horse, cat, dog, canary, or other pet, as well as an emergency food supply for them.

We suggest that you store in your residence canned beans, canned soups, and canned pasta for consumption after the earthquake and during the time of aftershocks. Add to your supply juices, coffee and tea bags. For everyone, a suggestion is to store at least two cans of soya milk in case there are babies from other people who are in need. For those of you who are coffee drinkers, you can purchase pre-mixed

The
Etherean
Travellers
and the
Magical
Child

coffee. Others can purchase hot chocolate. Make sure that you do not forget to have utensils accessible for your eating and drinking survival.

A small manual blender, can opener, axe, crowbar, hand saw, rope, string, wrenches, pliers, matches, lighters and extra large plastic garbage bags are essentials. Have available some kindling wood so that a fire can be started in a safe area, as necessary. Make sure that you have clothing supplies for winter conditions, including sweaters, woollen socks, gloves and rainwear. If you have little ones, make sure that there is an extra supply of diapers.

Let us give you some other advice. If you have the possibility of purchasing a camping tent, space blankets, a large plastic tarpaulin, do so in order to create a shelter for yourself and your family. If you can't afford these items, heavy-duty plastic sheets used by painters will do the same. A battery-operated AM/FM or short and long-wave radio will keep you in touch. A supply of candles and one or two flashlights (preferably one per person) should be located next to your bed. Other supplies needed are a foldable shovel from an army-supply store, a Swiss-army pocketknife and scissors. Keep your important documents (eg passport, health card) in a plastic bag in an area that is accessible to you in a time of disaster. Keep cans of nuts, candy and dried fruit handy and in an easily accessible place.

If you are not in possession of a foldable plastic drinking container, a small empty yoghurt jar or a small plastic bag can be filled with water to offer a drink to anyone. Two sets of clean clothing are needed for people who live in warm climates so that there is always a change of clothing. A large umbrella to shade you from the burning sun is very necessary (one per person).

For people who live in high risk zones where flooding and tsunami are possible, purchase life preservers (one per family member), or a large rubber dingy, if you are able to do so. If you cannot afford either of these, you can take empty milk or bleach bottles and tie them together by the handles to create a flotilla.

If you are caught in a disaster, there are cans in nature which can be rinsed out, opened up at each end, and mounted on a small pedestal, with candle(s) placed inside. This can give warmth and light and, if you place a container over the top of the can, it can be used to bring food to a boil over a period of six to eight hours.

When parking your vehicle, always make sure the hand brake is on. In times of earthquakes, vehicles will roll.

These tips are provided to assist you in disaster preparedness. Being prepared allows you the best chance for survival. There is less panic and shock when people have prepared and trained themselves well.

*The
Etherean
Travellers
and the
Magical
Child*

Part 4: Future World Forecasts

CANADA – 1998 through 2010

The following are samples of forecasts which were originally prepared in 1996/97. They are offered from us–the Etherean Travellers and myself–to you as a gift, a gift of awareness of potential future worldwide events and earth changes. They are also offered to allow you an opportunity to prepare in the event of a disaster. We would like to say to you that if you see the train coming, step off the track! If you have lived, and are living, a peaceful and harmonious existence, then there is nothing to be concerned about for you are aware that life is everlasting.

Remember, however, that all things in the universe are adjustable and changeable. Mass awareness and a change in consciousness can have a tremendous positive impact on the outcome of foretold events. World War III can be averted if people change their greed and war-like thinking and become peaceful and loving, thus creating harmony and balance.

When giving these forecasts, we give our best time estimates for the given events. It is difficult for us to estimate, however, as our time is different than yours. There may, therefore, be some small variances in the timing of events.

CANADA – 1998 through 2010

- Rising discontentment of the people with the central government.
- Many people unhappy with the governing of the provinces of Ontario, Alberta, British Columbia and Nova Scotia.
- People becoming less and less trusting in Canada as they see similar political and economic developments in other countries (Mexico, Israel, United States, England and France) and how the people in those countries respond.
- Economical condition slowing down and nervousness amongst investors.
- Stock market decline in the fall of 1998 and then through a very serious crash, most likely happening in the month of February/2000. The impact to the market will be felt globally into 2001.
- Many people in economical institutions (e.g. stock market, bank-related institutions) will lose their positions from 1998 through the year 2002.
- Major and unusual weather changes in 1998. The most hard hit areas will be Ontario and Quebec in 1998 through 2003, and the Maritime Provinces in 1999 through 2004.
- Major flooding in Ontario and Quebec through to the year 2006 as Great Lakes will link with Mississippi and Gulf of Mexico.
- Major explosion could occur in Montreal in 1998 and also in 2000.
- Alberta and Saskatchewan will experience more drought conditions; major storms from possible tornado/hurricane velocity winds; thunder, lightning and hail storms.
- Droughts will create food shortages through 2003.
- Flooding in 1998/99 in British Columbia – Prince George,

The
Etherean
Travellers
and the
Magical
Child

Matsqui, Abbotsford, Surrey, White Rock and Richmond areas which will continue through 2004.

- Earthquake and tsunami risk is very high on the West Coast. An earthquake in the Pacific Ocean could affect the ocean shores in Victoria and Vancouver. The greatest danger of this is from mid July/98 through mid year/2000, especially late December, 1999 through January, 2000 and May, 2000 through June, 2000.

- Major earthquake activity from above Los Angeles, up through San Francisco to Vancouver - August 20, 1998 to October 4, 2003.

- Eruption from volcano located between Yosemite National Park and Mono Lake in California could impact Canada.

- Mt. Baker will start to 'sing again' at some point between 1999 and 2003.

- More and more health stores will close their doors due to the pressure of the medical associations, the drug companies and the government, who is under their pressure.

- By 2002 to 2004, monetary choices could be limited to credit card only through one or two financial institutions.

UNITED STATES – 1998 through 2008

- Sliding economic conditions. Same stock market decline as referenced under Canada.

- President Clinton appears in the news in an unsavoury way, with his reputation tarnished globally, as well as in the eyes of the American people.

- Three major court cases for President Clinton, one of which will charge that he is involved with a major drug cartel in Mexico.

- Other countries will have serious problems negotiating with President Clinton as a result of his reputation, creating major problems for Israeli peace negotiations with Arafat and the rest of the Middle East.

- Deployment of American United Nations Peace-Keeping

troops to go and hold the peace in Israel (March 7, 1998 to April 10, 2003).

- Deployment of more troops to Bosnia and its neighbouring countries where there are large settlements of Muslims, and where there will be more Moslem and Christian skirmishes.
- Vice-president Gore will be looked upon positively in the view of the American people, from January 28, 1998 to April 12, 2000. Do not be surprised if he becomes the next President, unless public opinion sways to having a lady President which would bring the USA 8 years of peace and prosperity.
- Possibility of a 6.9 to 7.9 earthquake on land mass in California and a 9.6 quake in the ocean off California from August 20, 1998 onwards to October 4, 2003. Eruption from a volcano, which is located between Yosemite National Park and Mono Lake in California, during the same time period, which will rock and reel the earth in the San Francisco and Los Angeles areas.
- Major cyclone, tornado and hurricane frequencies over Florida.
- Increased volcanic activity at Mt. Rainier in 1998. Fallout will resume at Mt. St. Helens before 2008.
- Major flooding in California will continue. Severe flooding will also occur in Georgia.
- The coastline from San Diego up to Vancouver, Canada will be totally altered and changed before 2009 due to earth changes caused by the polar shift activities.

MEXICO – 1998 through 2004
- Assassination attempt on President Zedillo's life during the period December, 1999 through December, 2000.
- Great riots and upheaval, with a possible overthrow of the government.
- Possible earthquake activity in Mexico City and the surrounding area from 1998 through 2004.

*The
Etherean
Travellers
and the
Magical
Child*

MIDDLE EAST – 1998 through 2006

- Saddam Hussein will cause more and more difficulties with the peace-keeping nations who send their investigative energies to check for weapons of destruction. This will never come to full disclosure.
- Hussein will manipulate international public opinion and do whatever it takes to hide his weapons of great chemical warfare.
- Stockpiling of weapons of mass destruction in and around Iraq, supplied by China and Russia, as well as those being supplied through German arms dealers.
- Major problems with the profile of Prime Minister Netanyahu, who will most likely be brought to the point where he chooses to resign. It would be advised that he do so before June, 1998.
- Major struggle to take place within Israel's own borders where there will be major upheaval, rioting and discontentment.
- More and more discontentment in Israel from January 4, 1998 to end of April 2003. United Nations troops deployed in Israel to keep the peace. Restriction or cancellation of any travels, especially holiday travel, to Israel during this time.
- Major skirmishes between Israel and its old foes.
- Hussein will escalate disturbances over the nine months from January 26, 1999 through October 10, 2001. He will make a worldwide threat during the period from August, 1999 through October, 2000, as well as in August, 2001.
- Energies building towards World War III beginning in the fall of 1999 and coming into potential reality in 2000 to 2003.

ENGLAND – 1998 through 2001

- Major problems, uprisings and riots on the streets due to economical and political conditions.
- Totally different government by the end of 2000.
- Major accident for Prince Charles in 1998.
- Prince Andrew and Sarah Ferguson, The Duchess of York, will have another child, likely a boy between 2000 to 2001. This will draw Sarah closer into the royal family.

- Major floods and strange weather conditions within England.
- Queen may end up with a chest condition which could be either heart or lung-related and which will force her to choose to take it easy (December, 1999 through 2000).
- English Royal House will cease to rule by 2007. In the year that Pope John Paul passes to the other world, the Queen will abdicate to Prince Charles, but he is never to become King (2001 to 2007).

IRELAND – 1998 through 1999
- Major turnaround in Ireland, where the people of Ireland will seek peace.

BRAZIL – 1998 through 2002
- Major earthquakes, and risk of tsunamis rolling in from the ocean.

TIBET – 1998 through 2003
- Major earthquake activity.

PERU – 1998 through 2000
- Devastating weather conditions, floods and earthquake activity.

EUROPE –1998 through 2009
- Major political upheaval in Germany.
- Serious floods and disasters in the Netherlands by inundation of water from the ocean.
- Unusual snowstorms and disastrous weather conditions throughout Europe.
- Major disasters with floods and flooding throughout the European continent. Great danger for the European countries within the next three years as there will be an inundation of the soil under the countries and under the ocean floor. Shorelines will suddenly disappear (2000 – 2009).

153

*The
Etherean
Travellers
and the
Magical
Child*

GENERAL – 1998 through 2009

- In 1998 to 2001, the Ring of Fire will be completed world-wide.
- The outer earth crust is in a state of slippage, vacillating towards a total polar shift. This is what is causing worldwide weather changes and earth changes. They are not caused by El Niño or El Ninja. During the time of Noah, these same conditions prevailed.
- The Creator—The God of Light—will descend between now and the year 2009.

We warn the people of the United Nations, and the United States in particular, not to be so involved in the Iraq situation for this could trigger all-out World War III resulting in major devastation to England, France, Italy, Spain and Germany. In addition, nuclear missiles and chemical warfare will be directed towards the United States, which will also create fallout over some parts of Canada.

Be aware that, as the earth changes we have spoken about occur worldwide, most countries will be preoccupied attending to the devastation that the natural disasters will cause. You are, therefore, advised not to partake in any war activities since these activities will also activate the outer crust movement more, and put it into even greater slippage. And so you may experience your polar shift in a harsher manner, as it is now already progressing towards this outcome.

We have developed a world map that provides dates and details of earth changes, new lands rising, and social, political and economic events over the next 60 years, including some of the more stable areas worldwide. The information on the map, as well as additional information on worldwide events and earth changes, was too extensive to include in this book, but will be made available to the public.

We are non-religious and peaceful beings. We do not believe that anyone should own or use arms of destruction since we are all about teaching humanity to honour, respect and uplift one another. We believe in a society where everyone should be alike. Our aim is, through education and communication, to reach the masses and to change war-like and oppressive thinking and behaviour, thereby attaining a true peaceful and harmonious tomorrow where all creatures great and small can live in peace with humanity. Our future message will be presented to you, in part, through the Cosmic Energy Experience as well as through lectures, workshops and audio/video presentations.

Anyone interested in learning more or in joining us in creating a new tomorrow, may contact us at:

E-mail: ahtmar1@CosmicEnergyExperience.com
Website: www.cosmicenergyexperience.com

Help to bring about world peace by walking hand-in-hand into the light and knowing that there is only one Creator.

The
Etherean
Travellers
and the
Magical
Child

Glossary

Atmospherea: A collective of energies that blend from the higher to the lower worlds.

Corporeal Worlds: The material worlds.

Creator: The source from where all life originates. Also known as the Great God of Light, Great Spirit, Jehovih, Mataki-ashi-oh, Oh Elohim

ditni dut'ai ts'eke: Direct translation for Thunderbird Woman in the Dakelhne Language of Central British Columbia.

Etherean Travellers: Beings who can take on whatever shape or form they wish, in the physical or non-physical, as necessary for the conditions they sojourn in. Beings who can travel at the speed of light, which is like your speed of thought.

Etherean Worlds: The planes and plateaus in other places of existence, to which one can progress.

First Resurrection: A place very close to the earth where those people go who have gone into transition, in order to await and be assessed as to where they will go to continue their growth. This is also the place where many of your loved ones await you.

Good Samaritan: Someone who is kind and good and is willing to reach out to those who are less fortunate.

Hada: The lower world. Known to some as Hell.

Looeamong: An entity who has manifested himself as Jesus, Buddha and Mohammed in order to gather souls upon the earth, the lower world, and onto himself. He had originally been a Lord of the Great Spirit, held in high esteem. He fell into great ego believing that he could become greater than the Creator. Upon failing to become as powerful as the Creator, he created another means of gaining power by creating the Jesus story, the Buddha story, and the Mohammed Story. If you are able to check out what has happened to the greatest library on earth, in Alexandria, Egypt, then you will become aware that all the Zarathustrian writings and the story of the true Joshu have been stolen and used for Looeamong's own purposes with the names of the holy ones changed to his creations. You are living in a time when the Creator will bring forth, out of the bowels of the earth, all truths in order to gather souls from all those religious/spiritual understandings.

Potlatch: A First Nations' event. A gathering of family and friends during a spiritual time. Everyone brings an offering for those in need. Others receive gifts from those who are no longer in need. Also a naming ceremony of those who receive their new name from the Great Spirit.

Red Planet: The planet earth. It is seen as a red planet due to its war-like nature. (Mars is not seen in the Heavens as a planet of war-like nature.)

Second Resurrection: A place where those go who have lived peace-loving existences upon the earth plane and elsewhere, and who have lived in the knowingness of their Creator. Those who are here have never consumed other living creatures or beings and have not partaken in the killing of the same. They are totally free of the earth's negative energies.

Third Resurrection: The true heavenly place, existing of Light.

Thunderbird Woman: The one who came from the Creator, from afar, to bring a message of peace to all nations. Thunderbird Woman is known on many First Nations' reserves as a messenger of peace and as a healer. She is of MicMac descent.

The
Etherean
Travellers
and the
Magical
Child

We, the writers from the Etherean Worlds and Thunderbird Woman, are in no way to be held responsible for how you on the red planet–planet earth–live or what you do with the material in this book.

Thunderbird Woman is currently writing her life story. Look for her new book, 'No Daddy, Please Daddy, No', in the future.